What matters most
of All

SMART ADVICE FOR
MOMS OF BOYS

Francis Fernandez

Copyright © 2017 by NOW SC Press

All rights reserved. No part of this publication may be reproduced, distributed, or transmitted in any form or by any means, including photocopying, recording, or other electronic or mechanical methods, without the prior written permission of the publisher, except in the case of brief quotations embodied in critical reviews and certain other noncommercial uses permitted by copyright law. For permission requests, write to the publisher, addressed "Attention: Permissions Coordinator," via the website below.

1.888.5069.NOW

www.nowscpress.com

@nowscpress

Ordering Information:

Quantity sales. Special discounts are available on quantity purchases by corporations, associations, and others. For details, contact the publisher at the address above.

Orders by U.S. trade bookstores and wholesalers. Please contact: NOW SC Press: Tel: (888) 5069-NOW or visit www.nowscpress.com.

Printed in the United States of America

First Printing, 2017

ISBN: 978-0-99873291-2-0

Dedication

This book would not have been possible without the mighty hand of God who has guided me, as well as the pen in my hand throughout the years. He is the love of my life, my shelter, and Abba Father.

To my parents, I love you beyond words. Thank you for your support, but most of all, thank you for the faith you taught me to have in God.

To my knight in shining armor, thank you for your example of Godly leadership in our home; for the encouragement to push beyond my limitations; for loving me and ALL our boys with all your heart.

To my boys, thank you for being my sunshine, my courage, my gift, and the ultimate peace that fills my heart. I thank God daily for the gift of motherhood and allowing me to be part of your lives. I promise that I will continue to pray hard for you, be your biggest cheerleader, and love you with the love of Christ.

Contents

Dedication iii

Introduction 1

Raise Your Son as a Warrior 5

Let Dad Parent His Way 13

Encourage Positive Allegiances 21

Help Your Son Find His Helpmate 29

Don't Put Your Son on a Pedestal 39

Guard His Eyes 47

Teach Him to Lead with a Servant's Heart 55

Empower Your Son to Face His Giants 63

Know God is His Ultimate Father 71

Learn to Let Him Go 79

Expect Some Fish in the Clothes Dryer 87

Pray for Your Son 95

Refill the Mommy Tank 103

Embrace the Epic Fail Days 111

Encourage the Value of Purity............................ 119

Speak to Him with Intention............................ 127

What Matters Most of All................................. 135

About the Author 139

A Day in the Life... 141

Introduction

My reason for writing this book is to share the good, the bad, and the ugly of what motherhood with boys looks like. Some of the greatest stories of my life have taken place while raising my babies. Through this process, God has also accomplished tremendous work within my heart.

I have homeschooled my sons, sent them to Christian schools, and even public school. I have worked part-time, full-time, and even led ministry. The one thing that has remained the same has been my intention to raise my sons for the Glory of God. I decided from the beginning that if part of my job description included motherhood, then I would excel in not only a being a good mother but also a Godly one.

When I began to journal the stories that appear in this book I could never have imagined that one day God would use all this for my good and His glory. I wrote this book out of obedience to what He has called me to do, believing that this would bring women hope, a sample of what life looks like raising boys, and a reflection of Christ.

Each chapter is written from a place of love, prayer, and direction from God. I share with you examples of what has occurred over the years while raising my sweet boys so that you understand you are never alone. In some home, not too far from yours, you may find another mother who is struggling, thinking she's doing something wrong with her boys, perhaps with no one to share the burden with.

Look around you today and invite a fellow mom over for coffee, a Bible study, or maybe just the gift of a simple conversation. When we exemplify Christ in our homes in every action, others will begin to see His glory. Am I perfect? No, not by any means. I hope that throughout the pages of this book you will find I am far from perfect, but rather a mother who decided to reflect Christ to her sons.

2 Thessalonians 3:13 says, *never tire of doing what is good.* Mom, do not tire of doing what is good because in due time you will reap the harvest. You will see the fruits of your arduous and faithful labor to raise a good man. A man who is humbled before the presence of God. A man who loves the Lord with all his heart. A man who is convinced he was created to do all things in his life as unto the Kingdom of Heaven.

I'm praying for each one of you as you read this book. I pray that God would grant you the peace to know you are doing the best that you can. That He speaks to you in new and fresh ways to be a mother to your son. Most importantly, that you know God created you to do this job and it is the best title you will ever have. Let's courageously raise the next generation of Godly men!

Blessed be the Lord, my rock, who trains my hands for war, and my fingers for battle; He is my steadfast love and my fortress, my stronghold and my deliverer, my shield and He in whom I take refuge.
Psalm 144:1-2a

Raise Your Son as a Warrior

One morning, there they were, jumping from couch to couch in the living room; all three of my boys engaged in a serious game of superheroes and villains. At the time, they had towels tied around their necks, swords in hand, and arms stretched out as they pretended to fly. One hopped on a chair and said, "I've come to save the world!" The rest of the boys circled the hero, their plastic swords raised above them. I stood to the side, the queen of the castle they were battling to win.

There was a knock at my door and my husband greeted the guest, beckoning our neighbor to come inside. Embarrassment filled me because this woman had recently shared her ideas on parenting "a good kid" with me. She had seen me struggle to keep my boys in check and volunteered her advice. Advice that said roughhousing games in the living room only made boys more violent.

I quickly grabbed my sons and whisked them away to our family room, out of sight of our guest. I was torn between continuing the game with my sons and visiting with my guest. I knew if I went into the kitchen where my neighbor sat, I'd hear more suggestions about *how to control* my sons' rambunctious behavior. I was a young, new mother, who still worried about what others thought, and who was still unsure of my abilities as a parent. I wish I could turn back time and tell myself how silly it was to allow someone's opinion to affect me or make me question my instincts. That there was no need to prove my ability to parent, and especially not to someone who didn't have sons. Most of all, I wish I had told myself that I was doing exactly what I needed to do for my boys—letting them be the young men-to-be that God intended.

> I wish I could turn back time and tell myself how silly it was to allow someone's opinion to affect me or make me question my instincts.

I can remember countless times while raising my boys, that people made me feel like I was a bad mom because my boys couldn't sit still in a chair, or because they were loud or because they came home muddy and scuffed. Other people pointed out how restless my boys seemed to be all the time, and how this was a reflection of my bad parenting skills. For a long time, I believed this lie.

I began studying preschool education, partly to understand my own children better. I read a study about child psychology that said boys were not designed to act like girls and thus should not be treated like girls or be expected to behave like girls. I realized that the people who had been criticizing my parenting didn't have any male children. They couldn't possibly understand what it was like to be raising one boy; never mind three of them at the same time. My job as their parent was to help them become Godly men, not boys who would cling to Mommy's skirt forever.

Overall, boys are misunderstood. People have this misconception that boys are aggressive, but the truth is they were built to be warriors. God designed them to be hunters, fighters, and providers. Boys are not supposed to behave like girls, because they were created to be men; not women. As mothers, we should encourage and equip our sons to be the warriors they were created to be. I'm not saying you should let them run rampant in public, screaming and getting into trouble. However, neither should we think there is something wrong with our sons because they want to turn the living room into a fort, dress up as a super hero, or splash around in a creek and get muddy.

All those warrior tendencies come from a deep need within which also explains why boys must release a lot more energy than girls do. On some days, I take my elementary-aged son to the park right after school so he can burn off some of that energy before we head home for reading and dinner. For my middle schoolers, they ride bikes or skateboards around the neighborhood before they head home for homework and our end of the day routines.

I remember the first time I enrolled one of our sons in a sport. I knew the time commitment it would take on my part, but anything was worth the chance to show him that his desire to conquer something was valid. At the first game of the baseball season, he sat in the dugout, his big brown eyes looking at the coach. The coach read off names and the positions the boys would hold on the field. Finally, my son's name was called, and when he heard the position "short stop," he jumped for joy. As he ran out to the field for the warm up, I watched the shift in his confidence, as his motivation changed from a simple desire to conquer the field to the pride of being part of a team. Mom was just happy he would be releasing a lot of energy!

Playing baseball, basketball, etc. teaches our sons to be disciplined, committed and confident, as well as how to be a team player. As adults, these lessons will provide them with strong work ethics. My boys have played baseball, soccer, and golf, participated in fishing tournaments, and even archery. Over the years, I have made every effort to keep my sons busy with some sort of physical activity. They are not the greatest athletes, but it has never been about winning or making them into the next Michael Jordan. I am far more interested in giving my sons the lifelong lessons they need, and helping them keep all that energy channeled in positive directions. Sometimes all their sports and activities keep me running from one field to the next, but I know in the end it will be worth it.

I also encourage them to take some risks. When the summer comes around, the boys jump in the boat and head to the ocean for days at a time with their father. Many moms tell me how afraid they would be if their sons were gone on a 24-hour fishing trip, but to me, there is no greater satisfaction than when they return and I get to hear them share all the memories they've built with Dad on the boat: the shooting stars, the rising sun, and the dolphins they've watched swim alongside them.

One time, the boys went shark fishing with their dad and one of them caught a sting ray instead of a shark. My son jumped off the boat and swam with the sting ray for quite some time before releasing it from the line. He stopped for a moment on a nearby sand bar to take a picture with it. The sting ray covered nearly half his body in the picture. When I saw the image, I could have very well reminded him how dangerous that was, but instead I listened and told him how happy I was that he was able to swim with that beautiful creature.

Boys were created to be adventurous, goal-driven, and passionate. They will try to climb over the monkey bars instead of slipping through them. Boys love a challenge and everything that it entails. They need to climb trees, hide in the shrubs, or just run around for hours. Through these games and adventures, they are learning to be confident in themselves, solve their own problems, and explore the world around them.

> Every man who has been led by God in the Bible, has in some way or another been encouraged by God to step out courageously and do what He is calling him to.

This is what God wants for them as well. Every man who has been led by God in the Bible, has in some way or another been encouraged by God to step out courageously and do what He is calling him to. Moses was called to lead the Israelites out of Egypt, although he didn't feel equipped to do so. Yet he did! Joshua was called to lead them into the Promised Land and repeatedly God told him to be strong and courageous. God asked Noah to build an ark. Although people said he was crazy and made fun of him, he did it, and by doing so, he saved his family. God wants our boys to become men who can lead; who have the strong shoulders others will lean on; to be examples to their family of strength and discipline. So encourage your boys to be boys, allow them to be warriors, and most of all, love them for all their boy-ness, just as God loves them, too.

What Matters Most: Things to Do

- Don't let the opinions of others affect you in raising your sons.

- Allow your sons to climb trees or build a fort. Let them take chances, even if it causes you a bit of worry.

- Find one sport he likes and sign him up. Many leagues take boys as young as four years old.

Prayer

Lord,

Thank you for teaching me that you have built my son to be a warrior. That the opinions of others should not matter to me. Please don't allow the negative words that may come out of someone's mouth about my son, affect my heart. Instead, grant me the peace to know that I am doing exactly what You need me to do for him. That You have created him with such an adventurous spirit that he is not afraid to follow You no matter what You call him to. Help me to enjoy him and his adventurous spirit, and encourage him to express this gift. Give me the wisdom to know him better and meet his needs as a boy.

In Jesus name, Amen

He who fathers a wise son will be glad in him.
Proverbs 23:24b

Let Dad Parent His Way

I stood in my kitchen on a bright spring day, watching my son fishing with his Dad for the first time, in the lake behind our apartment. One so little, one so tall; both intent on the lines they had cast in the water; the anticipation of that first nibble. My son, who was only four years old at the time, paused, and looked up at his dad with such contentment and joy. It was one of those moments you wish you could keep in a box forever.

A moment later, my son let out a squeal. His rod bent, the line tightened. My husband leaned down, coaching him; teaching him how to turn the reel and pull the catch in to shore. My son hoisted the rod, proud of the three-inch bass he'd caught. The look on his face as he showed the fish to his dad said everything. He was so happy to have his dad experiencing this amazing moment with him. That priceless sight taught me how important Dad was to my son's walk in life.

Many couples start talking about having children before they get married, or right after they take their vows: *What will our children look like? Whose traits would we like to see in them? What type of personality will they have? Will they have blue eyes or brown; be short or tall?*

But the big question we often neglect to answer is: how will we parent them? Couples often assume they know each other's values and upbringing. But it's not until after that first child is born that we realize there were plenty of questions we didn't ask, and even more answers we didn't know or couldn't anticipate. Nothing can ever completely prepare you to raise a son. Only God can do that.

God wants children to have two parents, because He sees both as equally important. Moms bring one set of skills and life lessons to their boys, but the lessons they learn from Dad are just as vital.

At some point, you will both think that the way you were raised may be the best way to raise your son. Or perhaps both of you had difficult childhoods, so you don't have much to draw from on the best way to parent. A son doesn't come with an instruction manual, so we do the best we can with the knowledge we have at the time. When you have questions or doubts, the best thing you can do is turn to God and ask Him in prayer what path is the right one. God will lead you in the process of parenting. You simply have to listen, and make those decisions together as parents.

Your son was created with a unique purpose and God has assigned *both* of you to parent him. Stepping back and letting Dad lead can be difficult. But hear me out, Moms. While you possess certain qualities that your son will need, Dad will bring the lessons your son requires to help him become the man God created him to be.

> While you possess certain qualities that your son will need, Dad will bring the lessons your son requires to help him become the man God created him to be.

So, step back and give Dad room to parent his way. I say this from a place of love and much respect. I know it's not something we want to hear or accept as mothers, but it's a lesson I learned in the process of raising four boys.

Today, I look back on the days when I wasn't so generous with my husband and his efforts to bond with the boys. I regret that I didn't see the value of a good father-son relationship earlier. My older son would have benefited so much more had I been more understanding. Because I have learned from my mistakes, I urge you to allow Dad to parent his way.

Before your son was born, God knew what he would need. That's why He made you both the parents to this precious child. With our son, I remember thinking my way was the best and only way to raise him. My husband is adopted, and didn't have a paternal role model, so mistakenly, I thought he wouldn't have the skills and knowledge to be a good Dad.

That couldn't have been further from the truth. Because my husband didn't have a father to play with or take him fishing, he makes it a priority to do so with his own sons. It has always been very important to him to spend time with the boys. He has carved out time to do what each boy enjoys, and their four different personalities means they pursue four different hobbies. Although he doesn't enjoy all the activities they do together (the boys love baseball and he is not a fan), he goes along and supports his sons because it is important to him. And he knows what an impact he would have upon them. He also knows it is what God wants him to do.

As Moms, we tend to be the protectors, nurses, and even the voice of reason in stressful times. We often step in and do it ourselves because it's easier or because we don't like the way Dad does it. May I suggest that you step back, have some patience and allow Dad to take his own approach? The boys might get dirty or scrape a knee, but that's all part of being a boy.

Has it been hard for me to step back and let my husband parent? Yes! In my early years of motherhood, the overprotective side of me wanted to be with my boys all the time. But as I watched them bond with their father, I realized how much they needed him too! They needed Dad to participate in their lives, and I needed to move aside for that to happen. We've done plenty of family things together but have each also taken individual time with our boys.

An essential weapon a mother should always in her arsenal is being patient and full of grace toward her son's father. Keep in mind that scripture mentions in Ephesians 6:12, "For we do not wrestle against flesh and blood, but against principalities, against powers, against the rulers of the darkness of this age, against spiritual hosts of wickedness in the heavenly places."

Therefore, our weapons must be spiritual in nature and must include peace, grace, love, and most of all mercy. Mercy is not giving the father what he deserves; but rather giving him what he does not deserve. After all, isn't that what God has done with you time after time? You must trust that God will keep and protect your son since he was God's before he was ever yours to borrow.

An important aspect of showing grace, peace, love and mercy is prayer. Remember that the key to any healthy relationship is prayer for that person. James 5:16 says, *"…and pray for one another, that you may be healed. The effective, fervent prayer of a righteous man avails much."*

My older son is from a previous relationship. I have dealt with my fair share of what I thought to be questionable parenting decisions on the part of his biological father. That never stopped me from praying about their relationship. Every time my son packed a bag to go visit his father, I would specifically pray that they would share quality time together. That the memories of good times they shared would outweigh any bad ones he might experience. Regardless of your personal feelings towards your son's father, try to remember he is still his Dad, and the one God appointed to him. Whether he chooses to do a good job or not is not for you to judge, but rather to pray for. So, whether you are married to your son's father or not, prayer is not only suggested, but instructed. Prayer will reach the hardest heart and the fiercest of spiritual battles. If you want to see a healthy father-son relationship, then prayer is the key.

> Prayer will reach the hardest heart and the fiercest of spiritual battles. If you want to see a healthy father-son relationship, then prayer is the key.

Just the other day we went to a state park we frequent as a family. The boys invited a good friend to join them to go fishing. They all stood in a row on the bank of the lake, trying to catch something. Their friend hung back, though, upset because he didn't know how to fish. He said it was frustrating to him because no one had ever taught him. Instead of allowing him to walk away and not be a part of the adventure, my husband stood next to him for the next hour or so teaching him how to prepare his rod, bait the hook, and cast it into the sea. Hours later, as we packed our things and began to walk towards the car, this boy thanked my husband for taking the time to teach him and for being patient while doing so. Sometimes, another child needs a paternal role model, and it's important to allow Dad to step up when he sees an opportunity to make a difference in a child's life.

My boys and their father go fishing, to NASCAR races and to the movies. Dad taught them how to ride their bikes, tie their shoes, change a tire, and even fix an air conditioner. A Dad's input in a boy's life is significant to the development of his manhood. Some Dads are hesitant or unsure; so, start small. Ask Dad to change a diaper, or suggest they go to the park together, or attend a monster truck show.

You don't have to be present for everything. Dad has been equipped by God to parent as well. Your son needs his father to be the role model that God has called him to be.

What Matters Most: Things to Do

- Pray for your son to have a healthy father-son relationship with his father.

- Make it a point to involve your husband with your sons. Start by asking him to change a diaper or asking him to watch your son for an hour while you buy groceries.

- Encourage your husband to find something he would like to teach him. Like riding a bike, fishing, or building something.

- Once they have found an activity they can enjoy together, support them in that. Buy tickets for them to spend a day doing that activity. Encourage them to attend a monster truck show or maybe just a movie.

Prayer

Lord,

I pray that You lead my husband in being the role model our son needs. Help me to understand that he is pertinent in his upbringing. That his input is needed in the development of our son's manhood. That You have equipped him to be the father our son will need for his walk in life.

In Jesus name, Amen.

The righteous chose their friends carefully,
but the way of the wicked leads them astray.
Proverbs 12:26

Encourage Positive Allegiances

It was my oldest son's first year in high school in a new city where he didn't know anyone. No one from his previous school, no one from church, homeschool or co-op: no one. We had just moved to a new city, far from his previous friends. High school is such a vulnerable age for young men, and having the right people around him was going to be important. So, I started to pray. I prayed for God to send new friends who would be a good influence, and that my son would be wise enough to invite these friends to walk alongside him in this new chapter of his life.

About a month after we moved, he found out his best friend was moving to the city where we were now living. His friend's father had received a transfer to that city. A few weeks after that, my son met another boy in school who attended the same church as our family. That boy invited my son to join him at the youth group meetings. God had answered my prayers,

> God had answered my prayers, and instead of bringing my son detrimental influences in his high school years, God had surrounded my son with good influences.

and instead of bringing my son detrimental influences in his high school years, God had surrounded my son with good influences.

Although we moved from that city before he finished high school, the boys have remained friends. One is studying at Texas Christian; the other is serving as a missionary in Brazil for the next two years. The three of them have continued sharing their lives and experiences, inspiring and helping each other. My prayer had been for more than just new friends for my son. It was a desperate call to bring him deep, meaningful relationships that would create lifetime alliances like the one David and Jonathan had.

The Bible says in 1 Samuel 18:3—*And Jonathan made a covenant with David because he loved him as himself.* The friendship between David and Jonathon was so much more. It was an allegiance between them, set in place by none other than God. It was so deep that David even honored the son of Jonathan by bringing him to the palace and showing the lame boy mercy. Later, David showed favor to Jonathon's son.

The Bible says in 2 Samuel 21:7—*The king spared Mephibosheth, son of Jonathan, the son of Saul, because of the oath before the Lord between David and Jonathan son of Saul.* Their friendship triumphed over all obstacles; even that of death, as he showed favor to Mephibosheth who was Jonathan's son.

Recently I was visiting a family who have three sons. The husband told me that one of their boys had made friends with a little boy who constantly got in trouble for lying. They advised their son that this friendship was not a good choice, but they left the decision of continued friendship up to him. The parents prayed for this relationship, and within weeks the other boy found himself in so much trouble that their son no longer wanted to be associated with him. He told his parents that he didn't want people to think that he was also a liar. So, he distanced himself and looked for other friends who shared his values. Why do I share this with you? Because whoever your son creates friendships with can either direct him closer to or further from God.

I've always made an effort to involve our sons in places like youth group at church where they will have the opportunity to create friendships with boys of like-minded families. However, we have never forbidden our sons to have friends that are not from church. On the contrary, we openly welcome any person they consider a friend into our home.

Just the other day I sat in my kitchen, surrounded by my teenagers and some of their friends from school. I sat there listening intently to their conversation about parents, teachers, and even girls they knew. Some expressed how they felt unloved by their parents for some reason or another. Mostly this was due to the lack of quality time they felt they weren't receiving from them or the fact that they were being shuffled from one parent's house to another throughout the week. I made a pizza, set it on the table, and listened to them talk about girls. They discussed their teachers, the ones that were cool and not so cool. The ones who they felt cared about their education and the ones who didn't. Towards the end of their time in my home I interjected a few thoughts. I told them that no matter how lonely they felt, their parents did love them. But there would be someone who would love them more than they had ever experienced, and His name was Jesus. The visitors listened intently, thanked me for the pizza, and for a moment, I wondered if I'd reached any of them. Then one of the boys turned back and said, "I like your house. It felt good to be here, and I will definitely come back again."

There is an ancient proverb that says, "Tell me who your friends are and I will tell you who you are." In a society of political correctness no one wants to be seen criticizing or pointing fingers at anyone, but the truth of the matter is that teaching your son to make wise decisions regarding friends is critical for a healthy adult life.

Sometime last week my middle son invited a friend over for a first-time sleepover. They watched a movie, played video games, and went outside for a little basketball. The next day at school, this friend told my son that he felt different in our home. When my son asked what his friend meant by that, the other boy explained. Besides enjoying the Spanish food I'd made them for dinner, he enjoyed the fact that he didn't feel the need to fit in with the rest of the boys in order to have a good time. He didn't feel pressured to be someone he wasn't around them. Instead, he told my son, he felt comfortable because the boys did everything possible to make him feel welcome in our home.

Let me give you a different scenario. Have you ever hung around pessimistic people? If so, I am certain that after a while of being exposed to their negative thought patterns and comments, you began to have similar thoughts invading your mind. Or, you found yourself saying things that you have never said before and your overall mood was darker and less happy. That's the influence of the people you surround yourself with. There's a reason for the saying, "a rising tide floats all boats." The more you surround yourself with positive, strong and likeminded people, the more you will lift yourself to meet them.

> The more you surround yourself with positive, strong and likeminded people, the more you will lift yourself to meet them.

It is important for your son to have the wisdom and fortitude to influence those around him by his actions; and also, to allow their good decisions to impact him in positive ways. This is why it is important to teach your son to make the right choices regarding his circle of friends. Having the right influences in their lives is a major key to a healthy upbringing.

Recently, one of my son's friends got in trouble for cutting school. His parents grounded him for five weeks, and didn't allow him to hang out with his friends. The first day off his punishment he came over for dinner and spent the night because he said he knew he wouldn't get in trouble if he spent time with my sons. My boys are not perfect by any means, but I think it goes to show that their friends are noticing how my sons act and are learning from that.

This does not mean that your son should have bias about another's financial standing, cultural upbringing, ethnicity, color, race, disability, etc. It *does* mean that your son should learn to detect and discern both positive and negative influences in his life. The Bible is clear on this point and it might be a good idea to share these verses with your son:

1 Corinthians 15:33—*Do not be misled: "Bad company corrupts good character."*

Proverbs 18:24— *"One who has unreliable friends soon comes to ruin, but there is a friend who sticks closer than a brother."*

Proverbs 22:24-25— *"Do not make friends with a hot-tempered person, do not associate with one easily angered, or you may learn their ways and get yourself ensnared."*

Proverbs 13:20— *"Walk with the wise and become wise, for a companion of fools suffers harm."*

Begin by praying for God to bring good alliances into their lives. Pray He will give you the tools to teach them to choose those that will help them walk in wise counsel and those who will help them to bear good fruit. As the Bible says in Galatians 5:22—*But the Holy Spirit produces this kind of fruit in our lives: love, joy, peace, patience, kindness, goodness, faithfulness*, the fruits of those around him will also grow within your son, so help him choose wisely.

What Matters Most: Things to Do

- Pick a day this week to invite your son to lunch and discuss who he considers friends in his life.

- Have him write down three ways they influence him to do good.

- Reflect with him on these answers and discuss if maybe it's time to pray for those influences.

- Plan to invite his friends over for pizza over the weekend and get to know them.

Prayer

Lord,

Allow my son to select his friends carefully throughout his life. Friends that draw him closer to You and not further away. Friends that bring lifetime alliances for Your kingdom's purpose. May my son not forsake friendships but rather draw those in his life to You as well. Bring Godly friendships into his life, and put him in places where he will meet people who fit Your plan. People who will sharpen him. People who will bring value to who he was created to be. I pray that no matter where he lives or how old he becomes; my son may find friends sent from Your throne.

In Jesus name, Amen.

> ***Therefore, shall a man leave his father and his mother, and shall cleave unto his wife: and they shall be one flesh***
> ***Genesis 2:24***

Help Your Son Find His Helpmate

One Valentine's Day, I was walking around the local grocery store with my first grader. We discussed his day at school as I picked up a few things for dinner. My son paused by the aisle with all the bright heart-shaped balloons, flowers, and chocolate. He walked over to a small decorated box of chocolates, picked it up and said, "Do you think Victoria would like this?"

I stopped in the middle of the aisle. Had I heard him, right? Did he really want to buy a gift for a girl for Valentine's Day? My first grader had his first crush and this Momma was nowhere near ready to have that conversation.

I stood there, with a rotisserie chicken cooling in my cart, and realized several things. One day, my son would grow up to be a man, and I wanted to be sure he became a man with kind gestures in his heart. I could decide to be this girl's arch nemesis or I could begin to pray for the woman who would someday be his wife, even though that day was many years in the future. I could brush off my son's interest and tell him, "Oh, you'll meet plenty of girls along the way who you will like," or I could tell him that God had created the right helpmate just for him and that she was being prepared for her future with him as we spoke. The thoughts that flowed through my mind in the middle of the grocery store came to me from God. In His sovereignty, He was preparing this Momma's heart for what was to come.

No Mom ever wants to think that her baby boy will grow up, much less get married. But they will, and the best thing we can do is learn how to prepare them for that helpmate. The dictionary defines the word "helpmate" as: *a helpful companion or partner, especially one's husband or wife*. I paused that day in the grocery store to share with my son what a helpmate was. That day, I gave him a simple definition, and in the following days, weeks, months and years, I began to show what a helpmate was in our home. For our children, our marriages are their first example.

Every aspect of our lives is an example to our children and you have to decide what kind of example you want to be. By allowing our sons to watch us pray, read the Bible, and serve God together as a couple, our boys will in turn see that it takes work to make a marriage run smoothly. When my sons see their father and I pray together, they understand that we are inviting God into our home. That we are seeking Him to guide the decisions we make, and that ultimately God remains the center of unity in our home. As Psalm 133:1 says, *let us dwell together in unity*. When they see us reading the Bible together, they see that we are seeking Biblical knowledge to strengthen our marriage. That the word of God is a lamp unto our feet, and a light on our path as we walk our lives with Him. When they see us serving together, they understand we are a team that works together in all aspects of life.

In all these moments, we are teaching our sons that God is the most important thing in our home, and they see we are being good helpmates to each other.

No couple is perfect, and no couple lives a life without strife, especially with the stress of jobs, kids and bills. Instead of painting my marriage with the brush of an idealist, I've been honest with my boys and told them many times that we are just two imperfect people put together by a perfect God.

I cannot stress enough that the image you are portraying to your sons at home will shape their image of what a marriage is supposed to look like. If they constantly hear you complaining, being sarcastic, or even visibly showing how discontented you are in your marriage and with your husband, then chances are they will have the same perception towards their mate and the institution of marriage. The very thing you are trying to avoid in their life through your actions and words, will become the catalyst that could ruin the marriage God intended them to have.

Genesis 2: 18-22 reads, *And the Lord God said, "It is not good that man should be alone; I will make him a helper comparable to him." Out of the ground the Lord God formed every beast of the field and every bird of the air, and brought them to Adam to see what he would call them. And whatever Adam called each living creature; that was its name. So Adam gave names to all cattle, to the birds of the air, and to every beast of the field. But for Adam there was not found a helper comparable to him.*

And the Lord God caused a deep sleep to fall on Adam, and he slept; and He took one of his ribs, and closed up the flesh in its place. Then the rib which the Lord God had taken from man He made into a woman, and He brought her to the man.

When it came time for God to find Adam a mate, there were no suitable mates that nature could provide; therefore, the Word of God said that He created one for him. In other words, substitutes are not good enough: God wants the best, or nothing at all for your son. The next time you think that society, the world, church, school or any other "substitute" can provide your son with the perfect mate, think again, because God has already created the perfect future wife for your son. Prayer will bring forth that perfect mate that He is preparing, shaping, and forming just for your young man.

My husband has truly been my helpmate hundreds of times over the years we have been married. Being a helpmate is about much more, though, than throwing in a load of laundry or helping clean up from dinner. It's about being there for the scary, emotional times, and being a rock when I need one most. Our second son was born with breathing complications and was in the NICU. I was lying in my hospital bed, exhausted, when I felt a sudden rush in my body. A second later, I realized I was hemorrhaging. Instead of panicking, my husband rushed me to the bathroom and called for help. I was terrified, but he stayed with me, calming me down, praying for me and holding my hand. He didn't leave my side until I was in the hands of the doctors and out of immediate danger. On that day, I realized I could depend on my husband, even in the direst situations.

When I met my husband, I was a single mom with a three-year-old son. I had given up on finding "the perfect mate." Instead I started to pray for "him". I prayed for a man after God's own heart, a man who wanted to serve God with all his heart, and a man who would love my son as his own. Almost a year after I started praying for him, I met my husband, and within five months we were married. Ironically, he had been praying for a wife to come into his life as well. My husband told me shortly after we met that he knew right away I would be his wife. Even though we got married pretty soon after meeting, we never felt rushed because we knew we were made for each other, that we were meant to be each other's helpmates. We prayed every step of the way of our courtship for confirmation from God that we were making the right choices in His eyes.

I have always told my sons that being a team in a marriage is very important. I have come up with this acronym for TEAM to help us pray for specifics in our sons' future marriages:

Trust: This is the most important bond in marriage. May it never be broken.

Effort: May every day be filled with effort towards the marriage and His will in their lives.

Alliance: May they build a strong alliance together to bring glory to God.

Mate: May they both know that they are life partners, created for each other.

That Valentine's Day, my son gave Victoria a heart-shaped box of chocolates and some fresh-cut flowers from our garden. Although many, many years have passed since that event, he is still very thoughtful, caring, and kind towards the women in his life. Recently, my son and his helpmate celebrated their nine-month anniversary. He prepared a special picnic at the park where they enjoyed lunch and fellowship in the Word.

God intended for us to be paired with the person who will bring out the best in us and be there for us when we need them most. If your son is struggling to meet the one God intended for him, give it up in prayer. Ask God to work on that person who has yet to arrive, and to prepare your son's heart for this life-changing meeting. In due time, God will bring the two of them together, and create the union He has always intended.

> God intended for us to be paired with the person who will bring out the best in us and be there for us when we need them most.

What Matters Most: Things to Do

- Pray for the woman who will one day be your son's wife.

- Remember your marriage will be his example. Try to do everything in your power to exemplify a good marriage.

- Discuss other examples of powerful marriages or relationships, as examples of what your son should look for.

- Encourage your son to pray for the woman God has intended for him.

- Praise your son when he demonstrates small gestures of kindness to any girl, once he has openly expressed interest in her.

Prayer

I love the story of Abraham sending out his servant to seek a wife for Isaac because He gave his servant specific instructions. The prayer I share with you is part of one I wrote for my sons. As you can see I haven't been specific about her looks; but rather her heart. I have been specific about my request for my sons' future brides. I share this so you understand that you too can prepare him for his helpmate.

Lord,

I pray for the helpmate you have created for my son. I pray for her as You prepare her to walk life with my son. I pray that You will send her at the perfect time and will give them both a clear leading from You. I pray that she will be submissive to Your voice when the time comes to making a marriage decision. Let it be a woman after Your own heart who is humbled before Your presence. A devoted servant of Your house who loves You and walks in Your ways. Let her be the helpmate that he needs and the best friend that his heart desires. Let their union be forever and let the word divorce never come out of their mouths. May they be mutually loyal, compassionate, considerate, sensitive, respectful, affectionate, forgiving, supportive, caring and loving all the days of their lives.

In Jesus name, Amen.

"You shall have no other gods before me."
Deuteronomy 5:7

Don't Put Your Son on a Pedestal

It was an ordinary day at my house, and I was doing laundry. I was washing my eldest son's favorite jeans, because he wanted to wear them that afternoon. I was about to throw a load into the dryer, thinking about how much I loved my son, when I suddenly heard a whisper: *What if I took him?*

I literally lost my breath. It felt as if someone had just punched me in the gut. I knew it was God's voice in my head. I was reminded of how God tested Abraham with Isaac, when He told him to put him on the altar as a sacrifice. Instead of crying or pretending I hadn't heard that whisper, I took a deep breath and said to the Lord, *"He is yours. You gave him to me, but he is Yours."* The Lord giveth and the Lord taketh away, and what He decides to do is out of our control.

Those were not easy words for me to say. One of the greatest joys I have ever experienced has been motherhood. The first time I held my baby was such a special moment. The joy I felt was almost palpable, and no matter how hard I have tried, I have never found the words to give that feeling justice. In an instant, my world became all about this baby and, why wouldn't it? He was my blessed bundle of joy sent from above. If he wanted a toy he got it. If he wanted a specific meal he got it, I thought he deserved to be the center of attention always and to everyone.

Before I knew it, everything in my life revolved around my firstborn's wants and desires. At a very young age he had reserved the right to first place in my heart. But I would not realize my mistake about that until years later.

> At a very young age [my son] had reserved the right to first place in my heart. But I would not realize my mistake about that until years later.

In that moment in front of the dryer, I knew I had placed my child on a pedestal in my heart. A place that solely belongs to my Heavenly Father. There were many excuses I could have given God as to why I loved my son that much and felt he deserved that pedestal. I felt sorry for him because his Dad left us. I went through lots of trials with him during my single-mom years. I tried to compensate for the love I believed he didn't have from his earthly father. The list went on and on. But at that moment in the laundry room, I knew God was trying to teach me, His beloved child, a valuable lesson about who should come first in my heart.

My second lesson came through God's question. Would I relinquish my child to Him, the One whom created all of us? God wasn't looking to share first place in my heart with anyone, not even the very child He'd sent me. He was giving me the chance to correct my thinking. Don't get me wrong, I love my children with Momma bear fierceness. Now I do so, however, from a place of freedom. I am assured that God loves them more than I could ever fathom. That He entrusted me to be their mother for a specific purpose, but ultimately, He, their Heavenly Father has a greater plan for their lives that I have graciously been given the opportunity to be part of.

Putting your child on a pedestal can also mean making him the constant center of attention. One summer, we decided to let our youngest son dictate where we would go on family outings. Our excuse was that he was the baby and whatever he wanted to do we would cater to. This came to a screeching halt when we realized we were doing him more harm than good. If he didn't get his way then his attitude ruined our time. We quickly learned that a child should never make any decisions in a home. That is the parents' job to do together and decide what is best for the family. Our intentions were good, but in the execution, we realized why God tells us that He must always be first in our lives.

In the manner that Abraham took Isaac to the altar as a sacrifice before God, I chose to do the same that day in the laundry room. I surrendered my son before

Him, assured that He created him for a purpose that I got to be part of, that He loved him more than I ever could, and that no one should ever take the place of God in my heart. God did not take my son from me, but He did remind me of the importance of being vigilant to who is first in my heart, which I believe could have been the lesson he was imparting to Abraham on that altar.

When I was a young mother, my mother would say, "Kids are raised for the world, not for ourselves." In other words, they are raised to become independent and have the ability to experience life without you. I thank her for that advice now, especially since my oldest son has moved out and begun a new life of his own. I know I raised him to the best of my abilities, and for God's purpose. I have peace in knowing that God loves and watches over him better than I ever could. Whatever decisions my son makes from here on out I know will be based on the freedom I gave him to be the man God intended him to be. So, mothers, try to remember to put God first and your children second. Teach them that our first purpose is to the Lord, and everything after that will fall into place, according to His plan.

Isaiah 42:8 reads *"I am the LORD: that is my name: and my glory will I not give to another."* As parents, we must understand that God cannot share his Glory with any created being. Doing so is contrary to everything that He is. In the Old Testament story of 1 Kings 18:38, Elijah builds an altar, and at the

Lord's command he soaks it in water. After he prays *"... the fire of the LORD fell, and consumed the burnt sacrifice, and the wood, and the stones, and the dust, and licked up the water that was in the trench."* You see, anything you place in the altar of the Lord *will* be consumed. That is why He does not want anything to be placed there other than Himself.

This not only applies to children but also to any other relationship in your life. Whether you are married or not, no one being or thing should ever take the place of God in your heart. I've learned the hard way that He will not share first place with anyone or thing in my heart. Whether it has been my husband, children, family, or career: Anything that I have tried to worship or give importance to other than Him, He has either distanced or removed from my life. Don't grip anything so hard that He can't give you anything else to hold. You should not place any created thing (person or object) in the throne of your heart. If you start your day with God, and seek Him throughout, this will help you keep that reminder in your heart. You must model that same lesson to your children, teaching them always to keep God at the center of their lives.

Recently, we went to visit some friends in another city where they pastor at a church. While we were visiting, they invited us to volunteer at their food bank. One of our sons didn't want to go, saying he felt it would be a waste of his day. His reluctance only reinforced our decision to go, and to bring him. We took our entire family to assist this group of pastors. Later in the day, that same son carried on conversations with and was the quickest to hand the food boxes to the families entering the food bank. Later, he said he was wrong for thinking it would be a waste of his time and he thanked us for making him go. He said volunteering there made him realize how much we take for granted in our lives.

I believe in giving our sons opportunities to serve the less fortunate. In doing so, they are able to understand that what they have is a gift of God's good mercy and not something they deserve or are entitled to. Our smallest example could be their greatest lesson of leading a selfless life.

> Our smallest example could be their greatest lesson of leading a selfless life.

About seven years ago we felt God was calling us to the missionary field. We packed up our boys and our belongings, and headed for a new country. We really didn't know exactly what we would do there but knew God was calling us to it, and He would show us our purpose when we arrived. We spent the next year preaching the gospel, helping teens get off the streets, and really aiding those less fortunate than us. That time in missionary work was an immense life lesson to our boys. They recall each teen they met and how impactful it was to simply invite them into our home for a meal. Although they were very young at the time we served in the field, our boys have carried those memories of the less fortunate and their situations with them as a reminder of the verse in Matthew 6:33, *But seek first his kingdom and his righteousness, and all these things will be given to you as well.*

Your son was entrusted to you for a greater purpose than you can imagine. He is not yours to keep nor make a god of. That weight should never be placed on anyone's shoulders and it creates a dynamic where your son begins to expect that you will always be at his beck and call and that the world will serve him, rather than the opposite. Difficult as it may be, God should be first and your son second on the pedestal of your heart.

What Matters Most: Things to Do

- 🐟 Begin by admitting you must release your child to God.

- 🐟 When your child is demanding something from you, remind him God doesn't always give us what we want.

- 🐟 Do regular activities to help the less fortunate so your son will realize how fortunate he is.

- 🐟 Lead by example by keeping God at the forefront of your lives.

Prayer

Lord,

Give me the strength to surrender my son to You on a daily basis. To be comforted in knowing You have created him for a specific purpose and that my job is to prepare him for that. That You love him more than I ever could. Give me the wisdom to raise him with the freedom he needs to become a man of God.

In Jesus name, Amen.

Your eye is the lamp of your body. When your eyes are healthy, your whole body also is full of light. But when they are unhealthy, your body also is full of darkness."
Luke 11:34

Guard His Eyes

When our sons were young, I attended a Thursday night Bible study at a friend's house. The first three weeks the study was focused on teaching us about men. Things that men wished their wives knew, things they wished their wives would say, and the things men struggle with in life. On this particular night, we were learning about how men struggle with the things they see. On a daily basis, men are bombarded with sexual images and temptations from the media, and because men compartmentalize things, when they see an image it gets filed permanently in their brains. It may take a man years to erase a particular image from his mind. I realized, as a mom of boys, that in raising this next generation

> On a daily basis, men are bombarded with sexual images and temptations from the media, and because men compartmentalize things, when they see an image it gets filed permanently in their brains.

of men I needed to be very careful about what they watched and were exposed to.

I started paying attention to the cartoons, movies, and video games they watched. I began to do some research on content ratings and how slippery that slope can be. It only takes a second for our children's innocence to be stolen. One image can cause years of damage to this developing man's heart. I started putting parental passcodes on things I felt were age-inappropriate. Video games have the same rating system so I made it a point not to buy video games that weren't age- or even task-appropriate.

My youngest children are only allowed to watch educational shows that are rated TV-Y or TV-G. The older boys can watch TV-Y through TV-PG if it has previously been viewed by one of the parents. All my children love going to the movies, so I take the time to research for appropriate subject matter. Why do we go through all this work? Because I want to provide "*Whatever is true, whatever is noble, whatever is right, whatever is pure, whatever is lovely, whatever is admirable—if anything is excellent or praiseworthy—think about such things.*" (Philippians 4:8, NIV). When we allow things that are the opposite of this into our homes in any way we may be jeopardizing the very hearts of the men we are trying to raise.

This new computer-driven era that has sprung upon us makes it so easy to allow technology to take over. I'm not trying to make anyone feel guilty for letting your son play with an iPad; but rather to let you know how important it is that you guard his eyes for the care of his heart. Early on we established that our boys would never exceed a limit of 30 minutes for any technology-related activity. We had the same rule when I was growing up with television because we didn't have phones, tablets, and all that other stuff we have now. In our home, my husband and I keep television and movies limited to the weekends, and during the week, we stick to sports and school-related activities.

As the boys have gotten older they too have learned to guard their eyes. They have walked away from situations where they have felt uncomfortable by what they saw. They have even mentioned how their friends have noticed that they do this and asked why it bothers them to see certain things.

In Matthew 6:22-24 we read that, *"The lamp of the body is the eye. If therefore your eye is good, your whole body will be full of light. But if your eye is bad, your whole body will be full of darkness. If therefore the light that is in you is darkness, how great is that darkness!"* There has been an epidemic as of late regarding zombie movies and shows which have captivated a large cross-section of our society. The conscious being absorbs the images being portrayed of evil spirit-driven "undead" and stores said images into the mind (rational) and heart (emotional), subconsciously calling fear and violence into the home. In our house, we don't watch shows like that. But the other day one of our teenagers went over to a friend's house where they were watching such a show. My son said he removed himself from the situation immediately because he knew it was wrong but for a few seconds while he stood there seeing if his friend wanted to go play basketball, he caught a glimpse of the show. He could not sleep for days after that and needless to say, I had to strategically pray for God to remove the fear that was planted in his heart. Remember, it only takes one second for your son to lose his innocence, so protect it at all costs.

> Remember, it only takes one second for your son to lose his innocence, so protect it at all costs.

Our son came to us the other day asking permission to download an application on his iPod. He told us that he could use this app to chat with a friend who doesn't have a phone line of his own. I researched the app a bit and after not finding any reason to think it might be dangerous, we granted him the permission to do so. A couple days later he heard a ding, signaling that someone was trying to message him and chat. He looked at the screen and didn't recognize the name, so he decided not to open the message. The person sent a second message which now intrigued my son and by the third ding he decided to open the message and see who it was from, thinking maybe it was someone he knew after all. It turned out to be a total stranger who was not only trying to communicate with him but had also sent an explicit image of himself. My son was frazzled and didn't know what to do. He sent the stranger a message back, saying that he was contacting not only his parents but also the authorities. His brothers advised him to delete the application off the phone and tell us what had occurred. I was grateful that all my sons knew the right thing to do, and that our son felt comfortable enough to come and talk to us. I know this may not always be the case, but it's important for us to limit these types of situations as much as we can, given the world we are living in now. We are not trying by any means to shelter them from the world, but rather doing our best to guard their eyes from seeing things they were not intended to see.

Moms, I can't express to you how crucial it is to protect your son's eyes from the evil things of this world; things which can contaminate their hearts. Psalm 16:8 says, *I keep my eyes always on the Lord. With him at my right hand, I will not be shaken.*

In what ways can we help our sons keep their eyes always on the Lord? I started with buying them an age-appropriate devotional. This allowed them to start their day off by reading the word of God, correlated with a real-life story. Since my boys love sports, I found a devotional featuring real life athletes sharing a story connected with a Bible verse. Every year I buy a new devotional for my sons, and every morning they start their day with a simple five-minute reading. As the boys have gotten older they've decided on their own to also read a chapter from the Bible daily. One of my sons likes the Old Testament a lot more than the New Testament so he only reads that. Our boys are not forced to read their Bibles; we have simply taught them the discipline to do so and they see us exemplify the same on a daily basis.

Our youngest son, who is in kindergarten, found a small Bible that used to belong to one of his older brothers. We found him sitting in a chair reading a page from it, he was so proud, and told us that since he was now a good reader he could finally sit and read the Bible for himself. One of our sons doesn't like to read, but I am still very grateful that three out of our four love reading and choose to read the Bible daily.

Your example is the secret to success. Whatever we exemplify to our sons they will mimic to the world. I was never a good reader growing up, but by the time the college years hit I had to read so much it became a passion of mine which I shared with my sons. They read regular books with imaginative stories that are age-appropriate, researched and approved by us. When they are given assignments from school we make sure it is something that will not go against the principles we are instilling in them.

Do they read magazines? Yes, they do. They love sports-, fishing-, and hunting-related ones, so we subscribe to several. They watch the Super Bowl, Daytona 500, and even the PGA Tour. They are as "normal" as other boys with the slight intentional precaution that we try to be aware of everything they watch.

We have given positive alternatives to the things this world has to offer them. We've opened their senses to keeping their eyes on the Lord and as Psalm 119:18 says, *to open their eyes that they may see the wonderful things in His law.* You won't be able to avoid every negative message or image, but being vigilant shows your son that you care about his spiritual well-being and his journey from boy to man.

What Matters Most: Things to Do

- 🐟 Get your sons an age appropriate devotional.

- 🐟 Discuss with your son why it's important for him to guard his eyes.

- 🐟 Write down and discuss one way you will help him to work on guarding his eyes.

- 🐟 Be prepared to discuss when he does see something you may not approve of, and how it may affect him.

- 🐟 Learn more about rating and guidelines. You may start here:
http://www.tvguidelines.org/ratings.htm

- 🐟 Allow only 30 minutes a day for any form of technology.

Prayer

Lord,

May my sons' eyes be healthy so that their bodies will be full of Your light. Guard their eyes from the things that could defile their souls. Give me the wisdom to find the ways necessary to shelter their sight from this world and instead point their attention toward You.

In Jesus name, Amen.

For even the Son of Man did not come to be served, but to serve, and to give His life as a ransom for many.
Matthew 23:11-12

Teach Him to Lead with a Servant's Heart

Years before I became a mother I worked in the hospitality industry. I attended years of training seminars, learning how to improve my service standards. At the end of my career, I found myself working for the top hotel chain in the industry. This company taught me something that to this day stands firm in my heart. The mission to serve others was ingrained in my mind and it became my wholehearted passion. At all times, I wanted my family and friends to feel that their care was my ultimate desire. I wanted to exemplify more of a caring Mary spirit while working diligently and exemplifying Martha's great spirit of hospitality.

Your Martha heart must be thumping right now, because that is a tall order to fill. My heart certainly was while I went through this instructional time.

Fish in the Dryer

In the hotel industry, there is always so much to do and it's easy to get overwhelmed. Over and over, management taught us to slow down, make eye contact, address our guests by name, and always offer a way to serve them. Sound familiar? I now look back and see that even then God was training my heart for being a mother, and giving me the knowledge to teach my sons to lead with a servant's heart.

> I now look back and see that even then God was training my heart for being a mother, and giving me the knowledge to teach my sons to lead with a servant's heart.

When my children were little I would ask them to repeat Matthew 20:16 which says, "So the last will be first, and the first will be last." This is a parable of a man who hires workers to work his fields at different times throughout the day. At the end of the day, the ones who began earlier began to grumble because he would pay everyone the same wage. They felt it was unfair that he would pay them equally knowing that they did not all work the same number of hours. But the man's answer to the worker was that he had the right to be equally generous amongst them. In the same chapter, we find Jesus telling his disciples in verses 26-28, *"Instead, whoever wants to become great among you must be your servant, and whoever wants to be first must be your slave—just as the Son of Man did not come to be served, but to serve, and to give his life as a ransom for many."* By having my sons recite this verse, they would be reminded that even Jesus served His disciples and we should be generous with our service towards others in life.

Blanchard and Hodges say in their book *The Servant Leader*, "*Servant leaders, who consider their position as being on loan and as an act of service, look beyond their own season of leadership and prepare the next generation.*"

I would like to think this is our mission as parents. It can be an uphill battle, especially in today's world. As parents, it's often difficult to teach children to be servant leaders. We live in a society that instills ideas and thoughts about leadership that don't necessarily align with what God says in His word. We must be intentional about this. In our house, we created chores that served many times as a lesson of serving one another within the family. Chores represent more than giving a child a responsibility; they represent the opportunity to serve and give back in the home. My children are not perfect by any means. Yet, in teaching them to serve one another first, it has led them to have a heart to serve others outside of the home.

> My children are not perfect by any means. Yet, in teaching them to serve one another first, it has led them to have a heart to serve others outside of the home.

My oldest son was about six years old when he started doing chores around the house. We started with simple things like taking out the trash. We explained to our sons that Dad serves by working at his job, helping around the house, cooking dinner some days, and even doing laundry. Mom serves by giving up her job to stay home and take care of them. Their ability to accomplish chores in the home has given them a way of helping the whole family, and shows them that we all contribute in some way or another in our household.

When our second son was about eight months old, I began working at a Christian school. He was in the daycare while I taught in my classroom. His teacher kept telling me over and over how even at such a small age she felt he could minister to her heart. I honestly just thought she loved him a lot. He was so darn cute, as any baby is at that age! One day she said he was lying in his playpen, and she heard him making cooing sounds so she walked over to him. He smiled at her and she said she felt the presence of God in that moment. My eight-month-old wasn't doing a chore, but he was bringing God into her heart, showing another way we can serve others.

On special occasions, each member of our family does something nice for one another. For example, if we are celebrating any of the kids' birthdays, their siblings will take on their chores as a way to serve the birthday recipient. If it's Mother's Day, all the children collaborate with Dad to make sure Mom doesn't have to lift a finger that day. We do the same for Dad on Father's Day.

When I was growing up, my father always said, "Your first ministry is your family." And, "If you can't serve your family first you won't be able to serve anywhere else." I admit that when I was growing up, I was a rather selfish child. This was an area in my heart God had to deal with. When I had children, I made a concerted effort to address any negative tendencies as soon as I saw a speck of things like selfishness, pride, greed, etc. I didn't want them to be like me, finding themselves having to deal with these issues in adulthood. All the knowledge God had been depositing into my heart over those years, I have been passing on to my sons. It was the least I could do as a mother. As Blanchard and Hodges say, *"Jesus modeled the true servant leader by investing most of His time training and equipping the disciples for leadership when His earthly ministry was over."*

You may think that as a mother of a boy, there may not be much for you to offer him. From my past experiences ministering to women, the one attitude that always made me cringe was the horrible mother-in-law joke that went something like this: "Don't tell me how to raise my kids. I married yours and he still needs a lot of work," I have told my boys the opposite would happen when they met their wives. I prayed their wives would one day come and thank me for teaching my sons to be the kind and loving helpmates God chose for them.

If my son's first ministry isn't his home, he will not be able to lead elsewhere. God has created our sons to lead their homes well and to lead others, too!

Noah is a good example of a man who was led by God and who, in turn, led his family. As Genesis 9:19 says, *these were the three sons of Noah, and from them came the people who were scattered over the whole earth.* They led over the whole earth! What an impact Noah made by being a good leader in his home first. His children reaped the benefits of his example for generations to come.

Max Lucado says if you reduce the human job description down to one phrase, it would be: *Reflect God's Glory.* That has been the ultimate prayer of my heart as a mother. No matter where my children are they can reflect the glory of God.

Reflecting God's glory while serving others can be as simple as what recently occurred between our elderly neighbor and one of our boys. We pulled into the driveway of our new home and saw our neighbor trying to cut some branches off his palm tree. My son ran over to him and offered to do the work of cutting the branches. Our neighbor was very thankful that our son had given him a hand and we were very proud to see him serving another.

Another way you can create servant leadership opportunities for your son is by allowing him to volunteer at places like the YMCA, Boys and Girls Club or even your local church. Our older son has volunteered to mentor boys that are younger than him, mostly at church but recently was even asked to mentor at work.

I am of the belief that if mothers (and fathers) would rise up and lead their homes as Jesus Christ led his disciples, then the world would be a very different place. If Jesus, with all of his might, power and strength, and also the One who could have called down multitudes of angels to serve Him, chose instead to serve those around Him in every interaction, then I am called to serve my children. They in turn will learn by example, and it's important to make that example a strong, Godly one.

What Matters Most: Things to Do

- 🐟 Teach your son that his home is his first ministry.

- 🐟 Write down three ways you can teach your son servant leadership.

- 🐟 Begin to establish small chores around the house that he can help with.

- 🐟 As he gets older, help him find other opportunities to exhibit servant leadership, in his daily life, and on a larger, ongoing scope.

Prayer

Lord,

I pray that my son would know that it is greater to serve than to be served. That in the same manner that You laid down Your life for us, we are to lay down our lives for others. Let Your servant heart be that of my sons. Help me to exemplify that our home is our first ministry and that we should go out from there and serve others, as You did.

In Jesus name, Amen

Then David said to the Philistine, "You come to me with a sword, with a spear, and with a javelin. But I come to you in the name of the Lord of hosts, the God of the armies of Israel, whom you have defied
1 Samuel 17:45

Empower Your Son to Face His Giants

My son was about six years old when he started experiencing some issues with fear. He confessed to me that he constantly felt scared, even when there were people in the house with him. At the time, I was reiterating the ABCs with him, using specific verses from the Bible that pertained to each letter. The letter F read: *fear not for I am with thee* (Isaiah 41:10). This verse became rather critical to my son over the next couple of years as he struggled to overcome his own fears.

Every night before he went to sleep we would recite this verse, adjust his night light, and say a prayer for God's angels to guard over his sleep. But it wasn't just bedtime that scared him. He was afraid to be home alone during the day. He was afraid to talk to new people. He was afraid to be put in new places or situations.

I was at a loss. How could he still struggle with fear if we prayed for God to remove the fear from his heart? It took me a long time to see God's plan in my little boy's anxiety. I believe God was teaching both of us how to overcome our giants. I had struggled with fear for many years when I was younger, and by working with my son, it allowed me to become free of it as well. This freedom would come for both of us in different forms but nevertheless it would come. The lesson wasn't about God taking the fear away but rather having us overcome it in His name.

> The lesson wasn't about God taking the fear away but rather having us overcome it in His name.

I love the story of David depicted in 1 Samuel 17:45. David was a young shepherd boy who had never been to war. He had only fought off bears and lions while tending his sheep, and yet he was determined to conquer Goliath in the name of the Lord. What bravery was demonstrated by young David in this story! What strikes me the most, however, is not his bravery but his faith in the name of the Lord. Because of his faith, David knew he could overcome Goliath.

We found freedom by encouraging ourselves in the Lord as the Bible says David did in 1 Samuel 30:6, *"David encouraged himself in the Lord his God."* We constantly recited scripture against the spirit of fear.

Like 2 Timothy 1:7 which reads, *"For God has not given us a spirit of fear, but of power and of love and of a sound mind."* Fear is known as a gateway spirit which allows other spirits to enter. Once fear takes root in your child's heart then the door is open for other "more wicked" spirits to enter and take hold. Pray for wisdom, discernment and power to always be attentive to your son's spiritual status. Always be keen to call out into the open what is hidden in darkness. Fear is nothing more than a spirit that has no power over us once we claim the name of Jesus Christ to overcome it.

I don't believe it was a coincidence that God told Joshua four times to be strong and courageous when he was being installed as the leader of the Israelites. God knew that Joshua was afraid but still, he encouraged him. Funny how God can use a lesson like that in so many ways. When I reread that story in the Bible, it was as if God was saying to me, *Francis, it's all right if your boy is afraid. There is nothing wrong with that and it doesn't make him less of a boy. So, instead of thinking there's something wrong or I'm not answering your prayer, find ways to encourage him.*

I did exactly that. To help my son, I devised a plan where I would write down scripture about overcoming fear on index cards and placed those cards in strategic places like his bedside, the bathroom mirror, and in his lunch box. The two of us were determined to work together to overcome this little thing called fear.

Over the next couple of months, I began to see a confidence rise in his heart like no other. We would still recite our verses, use a night light, and say our prayers before bedtime, but the growing security I saw in his eyes as we recited our verses was heartwarming.

> Over the next couple of months, I began to see a confidence rise in his heart like no other.

By this time, he was ten years old. We had just moved again to a new city and it was his first day at a new school. All day I prayed for the first teacher he'd meet, the first friend he would make, and even the conversations he would have in his first day at his new school. In the past, my son had returned home even more withdrawn; crippled by his fear. I sat by the window, nervously waiting for him to come home. Then he zoomed into the yard on his bike, and into the house. He burst into the kitchen, ran up to me and hugged me tight. "Mom, it worked, it worked. I wasn't afraid. It was such a good day and it felt so good not to be scared. I have amazing teachers, an amazing new friend, and lunch was a blast. I met lots of kids. I was the new kid but I wasn't afraid to tell them my name or why we moved here."

All day long he said he found himself reciting Joshua 1:9 which says, *Have I not commanded you? Be strong and courageous. Do not be afraid; do not be discouraged, for the Lord your God will be with you wherever you go."*

About six months later, my son found himself at the first baseball game of the season. New coach, new team, and a new pitcher's mound to overcome. I stood behind the player's bull pen watching as he put on his gear to go to home plate and bat. I prayed hard as I watched him, and right before he walked into the field I called his name. He looked back at me and said, "I will fear not, I will fear not." I looked over to his baseball bag and there lay the index card we'd made months ago with that verse on it.

Here are some of the verses we used during our season of dealing with fear:

There is no fear in love. But perfect love drives out fear. —1John 4:18a

Their homes are safe and free from fear. —Job 21:9

I will not fear though tens of thousands assail me on every side. — Psalm 3:6

For I am the Lord your God who takes hold of your right hand and says to you, do not fear; I will help you. — Isaiah 41:13

About nine months ago our oldest son casually mentioned he was excited to be moving out, but I didn't really believe him. I didn't think he had it in him to move out, get a job, and pay bills like an adult, when he chose to do that instead of going abroad for college. I heard him hesitate the first couple of times he mentioned it. This kid had barely had a part-time job in the last year so I really didn't think he would go through with this plan. But he proved me wrong. What stunned me the most wasn't the fact that he was brave enough to move out, but that he said he wanted to be a good example of courage for his brothers. He wanted them to feel that they could do it too someday. He wanted to be their model, whether they left to go to school or just because it was time for them to stand on their own two feet. He wanted them to see through his example that they could do it, too. He went out and got a full-time job, bought a car without our help, and even found an apartment on his own. He sure showed me that he was a responsible adult after all. I think the one who was most afraid of his move was Mom.

Maybe your son struggles with fear, too. First, I want to tell you it is normal for boys to feel some sort of fear. It doesn't make them weak if they do. Second, give him the freedom to express all of his emotions to you. Who better than you to help him deal with them? By teaching him to face his giants you are setting him up for success in the future. The mere fact that you encourage him to move out of his comfort zone will equip him with the right tools he will need when he is a grown man.

Knowing that I have equipped all my boys with the correct instructional manual to walk through life and encouraged them to move beyond their comfort zone gives me enormous peace as I watch them budding into amazing men.

What Matters Most: Things to Do

- Write down one way you can help your son face a giant.

- Write down one scripture to counteract that giant.

- Talk to your son about other fears he has conquered, and help him use those skills this time, too.

- Put index cards with helpful scripture in his backpack or lunchbox that he will find later at school.

Prayer

Lord,

May my son find courage through You as David found; may he not find fear in his heart because You are with him. May You fill him with strength as You did for Joshua. Give him the courage to stand boldly in Your word as he faces his giants, and in the same manner You gave Joshua victory over Goliath, help him to believe You will give him victory over the giants he will face in this lifetime.

In Jesus name, Amen.

> ***You are the helper of the fatherless.***
> ***Psalm 10:14***

Know God is His Ultimate Father

It was an early morning in spring. I sat at my kitchen table enjoying a piping hot cup of coffee while filling my soul with prayer, worship, and a devotional. In another room my firstborn child, then a toddler, slept. The night before, he'd asked me the same question I'd heard a dozen times in the last few months. "When will I see Daddy?" Every time, the words broke my heart.

I opened my devotional book and turned to that day's reading. In those words, I found a message about God being a father to the fatherless. As I read to the end of the page, I clearly heard God say, *I am his father. Release the guilt you carry that his father is not present; that you did something wrong to drive him away; that you could have held on longer for the sake of his presence in your son's life.*

Relief washed over me like I had never before experienced, and a deep peace filled my heart because now I knew that God was telling me He was my son's true father. God whispered, *although I've sent him a Godly man as an example, I am his ultimate father and he is My son.* I sat at my kitchen table, the book in my hands, and cried like a baby.

As Matthew 7:11 says, *If you, then, though you are evil, know how to give good gifts to your children, how much more will your Father in heaven give good gifts!* As much as I wanted my son to have a father present in those early years, he didn't have one. All I could do was pray for God to fill that gap in my son's heart and demonstrate to him that He was his ultimate Father.

You may be feeling that same guilt I felt that day because you are a single mom and your son doesn't have a father present in the home. You may feel the guilt of not holding on to the relationship longer for the sake of your son. Or maybe you are troubled by the thought that you did something wrong and because of that, your son doesn't have a father to go through his life with. I pray right now that you would be released of this guilt and shame, because God is his true father and he is His son. God loves your precious son like a father. He cares for him like a father and guards his very steps.

Psalm 10:14 says, *But you, God, see the trouble of the afflicted; you consider their grief and take it in hand. The victims commit themselves to you; you are the helper of the fatherless.* That was exactly what I knew at that moment. Regardless of the struggles, grief, and afflictions I would face with my son, God would be our ultimate helper.

When I met my husband, my oldest son was three years old. His biological father was not part of his everyday upbringing, so my son now looked up to my husband for guidance. I was grateful for this earthly role model, but I have never stopped reminding my son of the message God gave me on that bright spring day.

It is important for my son to understand that although his earthly father might have let him down, God never will. God is the everlasting father. He is the best role model a boy could ever have in life. He has promised to never leave nor forsake His children, and my son has held on to that truth.

Throughout his life, my son has gathered wisdom from each of the men God has given him on earth. My husband has taught our son how to seek God with all his heart, listen to His voice, and follow His leading over all things. He has also imparted practical lessons about how to be handy around the house, mechanically inclined, and most of all, how to be a gentleman.

Throughout his life, your son will seek a manly figure to look up to. Moms, there is no one better than

God to point your son toward. If they are blessed to have an earthly father and/or a stepfather present, let that man do his job in the best way that he knows possible. Remember there is a reason God selected each of you to parent this boy.

In the book of 1 Samuel we find the story of Hannah, a woman unable to conceive who finds herself in the temple pleading before the Lord for a child. Eli, the priest of the temple, tells her, *"Go in peace, and may the God of Israel grant you what you have asked of him."* In the course of time Hannah conceives a son who she names Samuel, which means *"Because I asked the Lord for him."* The Bible goes on to say that Hannah told her husband, *"After the boy is weaned, I will take him and present him before the Lord, and he will live there always."*

Samuel would not have reached his calling had it not been for the leadership of Eli. The Bible says in 1 Samuel 3:1, *"The boy Samuel ministered before the Lord under Eli."* Did you notice the word **under**? It was under the tutelage of Eli that Samuel would acquire the lessons needed to become the prophet of the Lord.

Although my older son did not have his biological earthly father present all the time, he began to lean more on God as his Heavenly Father. He has always been surrounded by great men to glean examples from—his biological grandfather, my father, my brother, my brother-in-law and, by his fourth year of life, my husband. I am thankful that God allowed him to have such great men in his life.

If there isn't a male figure your son can look up to, then I would recommend you point him towards Christ. As I mentioned previously, He is the only one who will never fail, leave, nor forsake him. If your son has a father or even a stepfather present, you may not agree with the type of father he is, or even question that he loves your son the way you do. But our job is not to judge. Rather, we are present to allow them to be a father to the best of their given ability, something I cover in the chapter titled **Let Dad Parent His Way**. I've seen both sides of this coin as well. All I can say is that as boys get older, they learn who they want to draw life lessons from and who they do not want to be like when they grow up.

Pray for God to send men of good influence into your son's life. Men who will support him and give him a positive direction in life. Men who will be a good mentor, like Joshua with Moses and Samuel with Eli. You may also find great men to mentor him at your local church, on sports teams, or at school. Ask the youth pastor at your church if he's interested in mentoring your son, or go to the coach of your son's athletic team and ask if he would be interested in sharing some advice with him,

Isaiah 1: 17 says, *Learn to do right; seek justice. Defend the oppressed. Take up the cause of the fatherless.* Mom, it is in your best interests to direct your son if he doesn't have a father figure present in his life. Do everything you can to point him towards Christ as his example. Don't be afraid to pray for a Godly man to come into his life as a mentor.

John Eldredge in his book *Wild at Heart* speaks about unfinished men, and how God brings men by His side and also to the side of young men, to complete the job their earthly fathers did not finish or failed to do. God will bring men to your son's side at varying stages in his life in order to fill in the gaps that their earthy father left. This is important since this will occur without *any* help from you. Do not force it, manipulate it or "set it up;" God does not need your help. He is and always will be your son's heavenly Father. Teach your son to remember this as he chooses who on earth will be an influence in his life.

I love this promise God makes to David found in 1 Chronicles 17:13: *I will be his father, and he will be my son. I will never take my love away from him.* What a wonderful promise for our sons to know that God is their father, and they are His sons. And what a lifelong reassurance they have in knowing He will never take His love away from his children.

What Matters Most: Things to Do

- Let your son know that even though his father is not present, God is the best dad he will ever have.

- Write him notes or share Bible verses that let him know how God loves him like a father.

- Pray that He would bring other men into your son's life that he could look up to.

- Look to male relatives for occasional encounters of positive influence.

- Look for strong male figures to mentor your son at church, on sports teams, and at school.

Prayer

Lord,

Allow my son to know that You are his Abba Father and that You dwell within him. That You have blessed him with your presence. May he experience the genuine love of a Father that You have to offer him. May it become truth to his heart. May You also bring men of good influence to his life. And may You use these men to help him accomplish the calling You have created him for.

In Jesus name, Amen.

For I know the plans I have for you," declares the Lord, "plans to prosper you and not to harm you, plans to give you hope and a future."
Jeremiah 29:11

Learn to Let Him Go

High School graduation was quickly approaching for our oldest son. He appeared to be excited about what life held in store for him in the next few years as he attended college in Europe. We were excited that he would be traveling abroad, and had been given such an amazing study opportunity. As his parents, we felt we had prepared him as much as we could for this moment. However, I don't think anything could have prepared us for what happened next. College was paid for, conversations took place, and the people closest to us were aligning in prayer for our son's future.

One night at dinner, our son announced he was praying for direction in his life. He wasn't quite sure that God was calling him to leave the country. In fact, he really wasn't sure what God was calling him to do, so he was praying for a clear direction. We sat there, stunned, trying not to lose our minds as his words dangled in the air between us. Instead of getting upset, we told him we would pray as well. We didn't want him to make any irrational decisions but decide only to do what God placed in his heart. To be honest, we weren't super surprised to hear this. You see, at an early age he came to us and told us about a conversation he'd had with God.

We were living in Massachusetts back then and our son was about eight years old. He got up one morning to get ready for school, got dressed, and headed out the door to wait for the bus. As he stood in front of our house and waited for the bus, I watched him from the window. He seemed to be talking to someone while pacing back and forth in our front yard. I opened the front door and asked him, "Who are you talking to?"

"God," he responded. I asked him what they were talking about and he said, "I'll tell you later." The bus arrived, and off he went to school.

When he got home later that afternoon I reminded him of my question. He looked up at me with his big brown eyes and said, "God told me one day I would go to Israel."

I was stunned. The night before I had prayed that God would reveal to my son the ministry he had been called to. I'd like to think that maybe this was meant to be; as Isaiah 41:4 says, *Who has done this and carried it through, calling forth the generations from the beginning?* Although he was rather young, we have known ever since that conversation that our son had been called to live a different kind of life. Ten years later, he still remembers God speaking those words to him.

God deposited a dream in his heart that day. A seed of sorts, planted so that one day God would lead my son to that land, to reap the harvest of his future. As Psalm 33:11 says, *But the plans of the Lord stand firm forever, the purposes of his heart through all generations.* Take comfort in knowing that God has a plan; a righteous one meant to provide the very best life possible for your son. Begin to pray for your son's future today and don't be surprised if He begins to deposit a dream in your son's heart, too.

> Take comfort in knowing that God has a plan; a righteous one meant to provide the very best life possible for your son.

When our high school senior returned to us after much prayer, he said he felt God was calling him to prepare for full-time ministry. Not college; not Europe. Instead, ministry. As I said, we really weren't all that shocked, because this was a child who had felt called to do more since he was little. We knew if he said yes to God, then He would make sure to hand our son something greater. Our son now lives on his own, works a full-time job, and assists in a ministry at the church where his girlfriend's parents are pastors.

Psalm 37:5 says, *Commit your way to the Lord; trust in him and he will do this: He will make your righteous reward shine like the dawn.* That is all we have ever asked of our son—to commit to the Lord and allow Him to lead him down the right path. Was it difficult for us to watch this opportunity for our son disappear right before our eyes? Yes, it really was, but we would not want to make any decisions for his future that were not God-led. We would not allow him to make decisions for his life that were not God-led, no matter what we felt.

Some people think that as his parents we should have made the decision for him. That would have been much easier than obeying what God was speaking to our son's heart. When you are faced with a decision like this, ask yourself: what would you rather be: right, or obedient for the sake of your son's future? As Proverbs 19:21 says, *Many are the plans in a person's heart, but it is the Lord's purpose that prevails.*

I know letting go is hard, especially for us Moms. Sometimes there's no choice, and letting go is necessary. On the first day of kindergarten for our fourth baby boy, the excitement overflowed in our home. Everyone cheered him on, we helped him get dressed, and then headed out the door. We jumped into the car and drove to school. The car line was moving quickly and it was soon our turn to pull up and let my son go in the building. As the van door opened and he stepped out, I felt a flood of tears. I quickly said goodbye and drove away, before he could see how upset I was and get upset himself.

For the next two weeks, I cried like a baby when I dropped him off each day. As I drove to work, I thanked God that my son was in a good school and had a great teacher. Still, it took a solid two weeks for my heart to let go and accept this new phase in my baby's life. Did I mistrust that God would take care of him or that he wouldn't adjust to being without Mommy? Absolutely not. It just took my heart a bit of time to catch up with my mind. Letting him go meant putting him into God's hands, and trusting that God always has my son's best interests at heart.

During those weeks, I had to remind myself of 2 Samuel 7:28 that says, *Sovereign Lord, you are God! Your covenant is trustworthy, and you have promised these good things to your servant.* He has promised you, His servant, good things and one of those good things is your son. He loves him more than you do, and He has plans to prosper him and not to harm him. Plans to give him hope and a good future. Maybe you are experiencing a troubling season with your son and it's hard for you to believe this truth. Mom, repeat after me: *God has plans of good for my son's life, plans to prosper him, and plans of hope for his future.*

Do you see how God can take the plans you may have for your sons and change them for His will and glory? Ministry was part of the smaller plan we had for our son but not the entire plan. Through all of this we have learned that His plans are better than any we could make for ourselves or for our children. We have always prayed that our sons wouldn't pursue

> We have always prayed that our sons wouldn't pursue world fame or riches, but rather that they may be led by God and never depart from His ways.

world fame or riches, but rather that they may be led by God and never depart from His ways.

Psalm 37:7 says *"Be still before the LORD and wait patiently for him..."* Having trust and faith in God will allow you to let go with confidence, knowing that the Lord who helped you along your life journey will also help your son become the man he is called to become. This does not mean it will be easy, but it does mean that you must trust in Him. As Psalm 28:7 says, *The Lord is my strength and my shield; my heart trusts in him, and he helps me.* Mom, trust that because you have taught your son to find his strength and to trust in the Lord, He will help him make the right decisions in life. He will seek God first whenever there is an important decision to be made in his life.

Don't allow anxiety about your son's future plans to overtake your thoughts. Instead take the advice in 1 Peter 5:7 and *Cast all your anxiety on him because he cares for you.* I encourage you when you hear that small still voice say to you to *"let go,"* then let go. Not doing so, or picking up the problem, situation, concern or any other ailment before God has dealt with it could prove painful at best. I can't say it enough—let go and let God be God. He will not let you down or fail your son.

What Matters Most: Things to Do

- Write down this affirmation: "God has plans to prosper my son."

- Pray for God to reveal to your son what ministry God is calling him to.

- Write down one way you will discuss your son's future with him, and ask God to guide your son's future.

- If you are having trouble letting go, then think of ways you can keep in touch but let him go a little at a time. For instance, deciding not to call to see if he ate lunch, or checking daily to see if he has enough money.

Prayer

Lord,

My son's future is in Your hands. You have plans to prosper him, and plans of hope. Speak clearly to him about the plans You have and reveal the ministry You have designated for his walk with You. Help me to trust You and know that Your plans are better than any I may have for him.

In Jesus name, Amen.

"Come, follow me," Jesus said, "and I will send you out to fish for people."
Matthew 4:19

Expect Some Fish in the Clothes Dryer

When you're a mom, you never know what life might hand you. A broken arm, a last-minute art project, or even…a fish in your dryer. As a mom of four boys, I've encountered pretty much all of that, but one day stands out from all the rest, and it is now a memory the kids and I chuckle about often.

It was a beautiful sunny day in Florida. Three of my four boys scrambled to grab snacks and hats, and headed out to go fishing with their father. Almost every weekend, their Dad took them fishing, and that time with Dad on the boat equaled hours of fun and priceless memories. That Saturday they left as usual, with more snacks than they needed, fishing gear in hand, and a bucket of bait fish. I stayed home with our youngest son, who was only four at the time.

www.nowscpress.com/fish

Later that evening they returned with enough fish to last us for a couple of days, and plenty of stories to share at the dinner table. Everyone showered, threw their clothes in the washer and then went about their evening. When I got up the next morning, I remembered the damp laundry left in the washer so I did as I normally would; gathered it up in bunches and tossed it in the dryer. An hour later, when the buzzer sounded, I opened the dryer door and shrieked.

There, staring me in the face was one well laundered and dried... *fish*!!!! I screamed so loud when I opened that dryer door that my neighbors probably heard me.

My middle son, a smart and clever ten-year-old at the time, later told me he had put bait fish in his pocket for easy access while fishing. He forgot to get rid of them before returning home, and didn't even think of it when he tossed his clothes in the machine.

Life as a Mom of boys is kind of like that fish in the dryer. It's sometimes scary; sometimes unexpected; sometimes hilarious. My husband and I have faced dozens of hard times over the years with our wonderful boys, and have learned to rely on God to get us through those moments. I think He gives us things like a fish in the dryer to remind us to laugh and to find joy in every day.

This verse from Psalm 127:3-4a sits over our fireplace as a reminder of what we have been given: *Children are a heritage from the Lord, offspring a reward from Him. Like arrows in the hands of a warrior.*

If you are a mom and you are struggling, remember as Ecclesiastes 3:1 says, *There is a time for everything, and a season for every activity under the heavens.* Everything has a temporary season. Those endless nights without sleep, eternal loads of laundry to be done, and countless meals to be prepared shall pass. Not that I am completely out of the woods myself, although now my older boys do their own laundry and make their own lunches. I can say, however, now that I have an adult son who has moved away, I miss those days when our three older boys were little, running around the house playing heroes and villains. Today, I savor every moment left with our youngest, reminding myself that these moments are fleeting and I must capture every second of them through the hugs and kisses we graciously share. Here's to more hugs and kisses, and less frustration when they misbehave—and act like the boys they are.

My husband and I are raising our boys not only to be fishermen on Saturday afternoons, but also lifelong fishers

> My husband and I are raising our boys not only to be fishermen on Saturday afternoons, but also lifelong fishers of men for His kingdom's purpose.

of men for His kingdom's purpose. They will find obstacles or take unexpected turns, but in the end, I hope that they remember that what is most important is following God's plan, and spreading His word; one fishing trip at a time.

We have exemplified to them that there are various ways of spreading the gospel; whether it's moving to another country as we did once as missionaries, feeding the homeless or simply taking the time to help a neighbor out.

I believe that the example of leaving the comfort of our shores to venture into another country taught our sons that God will make a way wherever He sends them. In feeding the homeless they have learned that God is their ultimate provider. In helping a neighbor, they have learned that you don't have to voyage very far for God to use you. As Isaiah 6:8 says, *Then I heard the voice of the Lord saying, "Whom shall I send? And who will go for us?" And I said, "Here am I. Send me!"* He is simply looking for a man who is willing.

So, whether you find a fish, frog, toy or marbles in their pockets, the true treasures you will find are in their hearts. A gentle "drive-by kiss" or cuddle time with Momma, or maybe even a smile from across the room, lets you know that you are, and always will be, their first love in their life. How you react to the kisses and the fish matters. Your attitude will set the altitude in their lives, helping them to soar. Therefore, learn to enjoy and embrace the silly, surprising, and adventurous times that only raising boys can bring. Proverbs 23:25 says, *may she who gave you birth be joyful!*

Life with boys is always an adventure. I recall a time when my parents were visiting us. We decided to take a little road trip to show them around the city where we lived. We stopped at a local pharmacy to purchase some snacks before we hit the road. As we checked out, next to the register there was a box of red plastic noses that were being sold as part of a nationwide fundraiser to help children in need, part of Red Nose Day. My Dad purchased several and gave them to the kids for something to play with when we got back into the car. My Dad then fell asleep in the car, and my boys, being boys, used those red noses to take funny pictures of their Grandfather. Not only did they take pictures but they also sent them to our family members as a prank. When my Dad woke up he chuckled when he saw the images of him sleeping with those red noses attached to the top of his bald head, the tip of his nose, and even on one ear. He didn't get angry; instead he found humor in what the boys had done, and now that car ride is one of their favorite memories with their Grandpa.

As you watch your son grow up, try to see what a beautiful story you are writing together. The next time he wants to catch a lizard, venture outside with him. The next time he wants to jump in a muddy puddle, go ahead and jump with him. The next time he wants to throw a baseball around, offer to be the catcher for him. In our family, we joke that our boys got their skills on the basketball court from me. I didn't know a darn thing about basketball and probably broke every single rule when I played with them, but that didn't matter. What mattered most to them was that I tried and that I spent time with them.

Very little is said of Jesus in his early years but one does not have to go far to realize the love and affection He and His mother had for one another. In the Bible, Luke chapter 2 describes His birth, His presentation where His purification rites were performed in the Temple, and how He was prophesied over by Simeon and then Anna. We don't hear anything more about Jesus until he is twelve. Mary had twelve short years to enjoy the adventures she shared with her son. Certainly, Mary enjoyed a side of Jesus which no other human being had the privilege to enjoy. Even Jesus laughed, cried, played in the dirt and, if you allow me this creative license, also very likely gave his mother a "fish in the pocket" surprise. So, enjoy the years to come because they will certainly go by in the blink of an eye.

Mom, expect the fish in the dryer moments and when those stressful days occur, remember your son is a heritage from the Lord, and that these challenges are nothing but temporary. Focus on the adventurous story you are experiencing with him now and the amazing memories you will have when he is grown and on his own.

What Matters Most: Things to Do

- Write down Psalm 127:3-4a as a reminder that *Children are a heritage from the Lord, offspring a reward from him. Like arrows in the hands of a warrior.*

- Write down Proverbs 23:25, *may she who gave you birth be joyful!* as a reminder to be joyful while raising your sons.

- Write down a funny situation you have experienced with your sons.

- What lessons did he learn from it? What lessons did you learn? How did you experience God's joy in that situation?

- Find a new mom of a young son to tell your story to. Share the lessons and the way that God worked through your family in that moment. That mom might be struggling today and may need to hear your words.

Prayer

Lord,

Allow me to see that my son is a heritage from you. That there is a lifetime of great adventure ahead of me in raising my son. That finding fish in my dryer or any other silly situation that may occur with my son is simply temporary. That what matters most is the memories that are being created through these moments. Allow my sons to follow You each day of his life and in turn become fishers of men for Your kingdom's purposes.

In Jesus name, Amen.

> ***The prayer of a righteous person is***
> ***powerful and effective.***
> ***James 5:16b***

Pray for Your Son

From the time they were born, I have prayed for my children. Like most moms, I prayed for their safety, health, and protection. I knew God was listening, but it wasn't until I shifted my praying into something deeper and more personal, that I could feel the power in the prayers I was voicing before God. And see the results in my sons.

We moved to Massachusetts on a cold winter day. We'd left our family and friends in Florida for this new and distant place. My husband traveled five days out of the week for work, which left me home alone with my sons—aged six, three and two; all trying to adjust to this move. I was an overwhelmed mother of three little boys who had no idea how I could help them and ease their transition to their new home.

I have always prayed for all of my children, but on this winter day, after watching my boys struggle with their new lives, I felt a strong need to pray for my second oldest son. He wasn't dealing well with the move. At three, he was old enough to understand that we had left the place he knew, but not old enough to comprehend why. While he napped, I knelt beside his bed and began to pray for him.

As I knelt, I felt the Holy Spirit prompt me to pray specifically for his heart. So, I prayed for courage to fill it; God's strength to be the source he could draw from, and for him to find comfort in God alone.

In that moment, a deep peace settled over me, comforting me, and assuring me that I was speaking the words my son most needed. As I left his room, I was dumbfounded with awe. It was as if I had just been handed a special set of keys that unlocked prayers for my boys. By turning my prayers into individual ones for each of my boys, and spending those moments beside them, I could almost feel God surrounding my children with His love. From that day forward I realized that praying for my sons was one of the most important skills I possessed as a mother. That day, I prayed that God would fill my son's heart with a love for Him that surpassed their love for anything or anyone else. As Deuteronomy 6:5 says, *Love the Lord your God with all your heart and with all your soul and with all your strength.*

Every night, I began to do the same for each of my boys. I would sneak into their rooms, kneel beside their beds, and begin to pray for them. I had always said little prayers here and there, but this was some serious praying. You know -- the kind of prayers that have you reaching for tissues, because you are pouring yourself out before the Lord?

As Hannah did in 1 Samuel 1:10, *In her deep anguish Hannah prayed to the Lord, weeping bitterly,* I took turns praying every night, Monday through Friday, in their rooms. I became specific about what I wished to see manifested in their lives. Every prayer felt like an investment in their future, depositing strength and character into the spiritual banks that would bring them through their childhoods and into adulthood.

For my youngest, I prayed for his character. As Deuteronomy 8:6 says, *Observe the commands of the Lord your God, walking in obedience to him and revering him.* My youngest son is the one who has always seemed to be in defense mode. He would defend himself against his brothers; not that they ever hurt him, but still my youngest felt the need to prove himself and to make his mark in the family. He is daring, defiant to some extent, and sometimes darn right stubborn. Because of that, I specifically prayed for a spirit of obedience over him. I prayed that his thoughts, actions, and words would always be under the authority of Christ. As 2 Corinthians 10:5 says, *We demolish arguments and every pretension that sets itself up against the knowledge of God, and we take captive every thought to make it obedient to Christ.* I prayed God would guard his mouth to speak truth; that he would have more actions of love and kindness towards others. And as Ephesians 4:15 says, *Instead, speaking the truth in love, we will grow to become in every respect the mature body of Him who is the head, that is, Christ.*

For my oldest, I prayed for humbleness to fill his heart. As James 4:10 says, *Humble yourselves before the Lord, and he will lift you up.* My oldest was constantly being told by other people that he was charming, amicable, and good-looking. I didn't want this to be a hindrance in his walk with God, or to become something that ruled his thoughts. So, I prayed for him to be a man humbled before God more often than he was charming before people.

Over the next weeks and months, I began to see the result of declaring specific prayers over each of my children. The more I prayed for them, the more God revealed His plans to be fulfilled in their lives. Praying for the spirit of obedience over my headstrong child is an ongoing process, and many moms can attest to the same. But as 2 Chronicles 15:7 says, *But as for you, be strong and do not give up, for your work will be rewarded."* My second son no longer struggles when we move but rather embraces it for the adventure it presents to him.

I look at these nightly prayers as if I was a farmer of sorts. I'm planting seeds of prayer that will not bear fruit right away. However, I know in the future my sons will prosper as Psalm 1:3 says, *that a person is like a tree planted by streams of water, which yields its fruit in season and whose leaf does not wither— whatever they do prospers.*

Parenting is about doing the groundwork, and part of that groundwork is prayer. I figured that I had an important job to do, and I wanted to do it to the best of my ability and with God's given wisdom. I have had the pleasure of raising the next generation of Godly men, husbands, and fathers. If I don't pray, instruct, and guide them with God's leading, then who will? Proverbs 22:6 says, *Train up a child in the way he should go, and when he is old he will not depart from it.*

There is a Chinese proverb that says, *"Give a man a fish, and you feed him for a day. Teach a man to fish, and you feed him for a lifetime."* I often think of this proverbial phrase because our boys have been taught to fish in every aspect; physically, mentally, and spiritually. Physically, they love the hobby of going out fishing with Dad on the boat and creating lifetime memories. They are ever hopeful that Jesus will show up on their fishing trip like he did for Simon Peter, Nathanael, and Thomas in John 21:6, *He said, "Throw your net on the right side of the boat and you will find some." When they did, they were unable to haul the net in because of the large number of fish.*

It's not just about literal fishing for our boys, though. Mentally, they know they need to cast their cares upon the Lord and He will answer them in due time. As Psalm 55:22 says, *Cast your cares on the Lord and he will sustain you; He will never let the righteous be shaken.* Spiritually, they are learning that they are fishers of men for His kingdom's purposes. As Jesus says in Matthew 4:19, *Come, follow me," Jesus said, "and I will send you out to fish for people."* Nothing our sons cast into the kingdom will be returned void to them.

I want to be like Solomon was before the Lord in 1 Kings 8:27 which says, *Yet give attention to your servant's prayer and his plea for mercy, Lord my God. Hear the cry and the prayer that your servant is praying in Your presence this day.* When we come in that posture of worship before the Lord, He is sure to answer the prayers being brought before Him for our sons.

Having the tool of prayer for your children, and for yourself, will remind your family of God's unwavering faithfulness and create a faith building experience for the entire family. As Proverbs 31:26 says, *She speaks with wisdom, and faithful instruction is on her tongue.*

> Having the tool of prayer for your children, and for yourself, will remind your family of God's unwavering faithfulness and create a faith building experience for the entire family.

What Matters Most: Things to Do

- Designate a time in the day that works for you to pray; and journal those prayers for your child. One day the journal will be a special keepsake.

- Pray for God to reveal to you the specific areas that are needed to intercede for your son.

- Write down the character traits you would like to see manifest in your son's life. Examples: obedience, humbleness, and purity.

- Pray as Deuteronomy 6:5 says, that your son may *Love the Lord your God with all your heart and with all your soul and with all your strength.*

- Pray specific scripture towards those character traits you would like to see in his life. Example: Psalm 1:3, Galatians 5:22, Matthew 22:37

Prayer

Lord,

Teach me to pray for my son. Reveal to me what areas You need me to intercede for, specifically over his life. Bring to my memory specific scripture that I may pray over him to see Your character manifest in his life. I pray that he would love You with all his heart, with all his soul, and with all his strength. I pray that my son's heart would be filled with courage, obedience, and humbleness. Allow him to be a man of strength and courage like Joshua. Allow him to be a man who walks humbly before You like David. Allow him to be a man who is obedient to Your instructions like Abraham. Allow me to see my son grow up and become a man who fears You. A man who obeys You wholeheartedly and is humbled before Your presence.

In Jesus name, Amen.

Whoever dwells in the shelter of the Most High will rest in the shadow of the Almighty.
Psalm 91:1

Refill the Mommy Tank

I woke up on Mother's Day in 2014, to a homemade breakfast and my children all gathered around my bed. They each had a gift for me; something they had either bought or graciously hand made.

Then one of my sons handed me a cute little mason jar filled with folded pieces of paper. As he handed it to me he said, "Mom, I hope you enjoy the little moments I've recorded for you."

Little moments? I have four boys. That could mean anything from the time I got mad at them for riding a skateboard in the house, to the night I burned the cupcakes I'd promised to bring to school. A little cautious, I began to open the pieces of paper and read. In a second, I saw that my son's memories of those little moments were very different from mine. Moments that I thought had been catastrophic were times he remembered fondly and could laugh at.

Like this one: "I remember the time you kicked a soccer ball and it hit our baby brother in the face. That was funny." I remember feeling so bad when that happened, and my son was right; his baby brother did cry as I scrambled to get him an ice pack. What I thought had been a failed moment, my son remembered as funny. He had dozens of these kinds of moments in that jar, from bedtime stories to missed appointments; all of them treasured enough by him to end up on one of those handwritten slips of paper. That morning, my Mommy Tank was full.

As Moms, we are often so busy taking care of our families that we forget to take time for ourselves. Boys, with all their busy-ness, messes and activities can make finding Mommy time even harder. I spend my days playing soccer or cleaning up mud, in a boy's world. It's important to me to refill my Mommy Tank so that I can be a better mother, a better wife and a better woman. We need to do this so that we stay strong enough to turn around and take care of our family. As Matthew 11:28 says, *"Come to me, all you who are weary and burdened, and I will give you rest.*

Rest is not only a necessity but an instruction we find in the Bible, in Genesis 2:2-3 it says, *By the seventh day God had finished the work he had been doing; so, on the seventh day he rested from all his work. Then God blessed the seventh day and made it holy, because on it he rested from all the work of creating that he had done.* You see, even God rested and made sure we saw how important it is to find rest. An overworked mother is nothing more than a hot mess.

It's important to fill your Mommy Tank and make it a priority for the sake of your family. I remember after having my third son, who was fifteen months apart from the second one, that I felt spent. Breastfeeding this baby every two hours, trying to take care of my then sixteen-month-old and seven-year-old was a bit much for this mom; not to mention running a household while Dad traveled for work five days out of seven. It was a Wednesday when I realized I had been wearing the same pajamas for the last two days and was not even sure if I had brushed my teeth. I remember waiting for my older son to arrive home from school that day, as anxious as a kid on Christmas morning. As he walked in the door, I put on cartoons for all of them, asked him to watch his brothers and bolted for the shower. I promised myself that days like that would never happen again, for my own sake and theirs. You are of no value to anyone in your home if you are not taking care of yourself. As Psalm 62:5 says, *Yes, may your soul, find rest in God; for your hope comes from him.*

There are several ways to fill our Mommy Tanks. For me, it's the small things that add joy to my day. When I had my first child, I made a list of everything I enjoyed doing before I became a mom. I decided to pick my top three and stick to them every day, as much as my schedule would allow. First on my list was spending time each day reading my Bible and journaling while in prayer. This has resulted in over ten journals filled with answered prayers, things I've heard God speak to my heart, and things I've experienced in life. Second was not giving up my love of books. Every morning I wake up before everyone else to read for at least 30 minutes. That way I reach my goal of reading one book per month. Third is exercise. I have to admit that this one has been a very hard habit to keep up with in the last year, but there have been seasons where I've run a 5K easily. I know how important exercise is, so I am resolving to make more time for it every week. I reminded myself of this resolution while writing this book, and have now set up a home gym in my garage. Guess who will be running a 5k soon again? Want to join me?

Ask yourself, what are the ways your Mommy Tank can be filled? There are no right or wrong answers here: it's what works for you. I'm sure you've heard the saying: if Mom isn't happy, no one is. Your moods, your inner strength, your confidence—all of that trickles down into the family and affects the entire group. Don't let guilt cheat you out of taking care of yourself because I guarantee your son would rather see a happy Mommy than a cranky one. This also teaches them that it is okay to take care of themselves; to

> Your moods, your inner strength, your confidence—all of that trickles down into the family and affects the entire group. Don't let guilt cheat you out of taking care of yourself.

work out or read or go to classes, so that they stay well and become more enriched, better leaders for their own families someday.

Allow me to share one last note from that Mother's Day gift. It said, *I remember the time you made delicious blueberry pancakes for me on a Saturday morning.* He saw this as a sacrifice, because most weekend mornings, I am tired from the busy week before. But that particular day, I had just finished running five miles and had so much energy, I could have built a house. I could have run off and done something more for myself, but I find that sometimes, sitting down to a breakfast with my sons is another way to fill that tank. And for my son, it is the love and effort that I put into making his favorite pancakes that he remembers to this day.

Jesus often separated himself to spend time filling up his tank, particularly after ministering to a crowd. We read in Mark 1:35, *"Now in the morning, having risen a long while before daylight, He went out and departed to a solitary place; and there He prayed."* We also read in Matthew 14:23, *"And when He had sent the multitudes away, He went up on the mountain by Himself to pray. Now when evening came, He was alone there."* You see, Jesus would separate himself at times because He felt He needed to be filled and grounded by the Father above. In the same way, I pray that you take the time to separate yourself to fill your Mommy Tank. If you do, you will be able to more effectively minister to your sons.

As I mentioned before, there are no wrong or right ways to fill that tank but I suggest you start by sitting down and making a list of the things you enjoy doing without children being involved. On days like today, when I have been writing at my kitchen table for hours, I would settle for something as simple as a chair by the ocean and a good book to lose myself in. What does filling your tank look like?

Don't be afraid to ask a friend to spend some quality time with you. I have found great comfort in spending quality time with my "sisters from another mister", as I call them. I have known them since we were in elementary school, and although they live four hours away, it fills my heart to enjoy some good conversation and a yummy meal with them. We have spent hours together, sharing our Mommy stories and laughing at some of our mishaps.

Maybe for you it's spending time doing something fun with your spouse like cycling, sharing a banana split, or even just a cup of coffee. Whatever filling your tank looks like, do it. Take care of yourself.

What Matters Most: Things to Do

- Write down this statement "Rest is mandatory."
- Write down one way you will commit to taking care of yourself this week.
- Once you write it down do it, within one week.
- Connect with other moms who need the same tank refill, and set up weekly excursions, whether it's a simple walk without kids or a manicure.
- Remember there are no wrong or right ways to fill your Mommy Tank.

Prayer

Lord,

Remind me that even You rested on the seventh day. That rest is mandatory for my physical and mental well-being. That I am of little use if I'm not well rested and taken care of. Allow me to make my time with You a priority. May I find rest in Your presence. Give me peace to not feel guilty when I make time for myself. Allow me to be committed to making time for myself so that I can effectively take care of my son.

In Jesus name, Amen.

"My grace is sufficient for you, for my strength is made perfect in weakness."
2 Corinthians 12:9

Embrace the Epic Fail Days

We were home wrapping up our morning routine when a friend called to let me know she was at our local library, and did we want to meet her there? I put the dishes in the sink, then told my boys to hurry up getting ready and into the car. The more I tried to rush them, the slower they went. No matter what I did, the boys just seemed to move slower. I could see the window of time available to meet my friend narrowing more with each minute. Twenty minutes later, everyone was finally strapped in their car seats and ready to go. I couldn't get to the library fast enough. I worried that my friend had grown tired of waiting for me and had gone home. We parked, and all the boys darted out of the car. All but one. He sat in the back seat, silent. I told him to come with us, twice; three times. Instead of moving, he began to sob.

"What's wrong?" I asked, thinking he was sick or hurt or something.

He looked up at me with his big brown eyes full of sorrow and said, "I can't get out of the car, Mommy. I forgot my shoes."

You know those epic fail days when you wish you could start over from the beginning? The ones you wonder if it would have been better to have stayed in bed rather than going through that crazy day? For me, I've had many of those days with all my kids. Having five kids teaches you to accept the epic fail days and laugh about them. In the years since then, my friend and I have laughed many times over that failed library trip

If you're like most moms, myself included, you are probably often tired. You may find that you are juggling work, kids, and taking care of your home (which might be a total disaster right now), but you need to cut yourself some slack and remember that you are doing the best job you can. As God reminds us often, *this too shall pass.*

I've had so many of those days. Like the day, I was working at home, catching up on some emails. I had to order some T-shirts online with my credit card. I did that, then rushed out the door to pick up my youngest son from school. After picking him up I realized I was so caught up with my day that I never had lunch. I headed over to a chicken takeout place and ordered some food for my son and I. When I went to pay, I realized I didn't have my credit card in my wallet. I stood there dazed, confused, and hungry.

The manager was kind enough to cover my meal when he saw that I was nearing a total breakdown. Such a blessing, for sure! I couldn't thank him enough for his kind gesture.

Sometimes I get distracted or rushed, and things fall apart. When we bought a new grill, I planned a fabulous dinner. I bought beef ribs, potatoes, and corn. I wrapped the potatoes and corn in foil and put them on the top rack to cook. I seasoned the ribs and threw them on the grill as well. When the corn and potatoes were done, I took them off the heat, and realized the ribs still needed a bit of time, and some seasoning. I lathered on barbeque sauce, then turned up the heat, forgetting about the reaction between flames and sugar. Five minutes later I saw flames licking our patio ceiling. When I opened the lid, the ribs were engulfed in flames. That night our dinner was a plate full of baked potato, corn, and BBQ epic failure.

Sometimes you feel like you failed as a mother because your actions make your child cry. It was Presidents' weekend and one of my sons would be celebrating his 12th birthday. Since his birthday was on Monday and there would be school that day, we decided to celebrate for the entire weekend instead. On Friday, family came and we celebrated with a special dinner. On Saturday, he went to an antique car show and the movies. On Sunday, we took him out to his favorite restaurant for a family lunch, and in the evening, we cut a birthday cake for him. Monday finally arrived, and he went to school as he normally would. When he came home that afternoon I asked him how his day went. He became teary-eyed, so heartbroken that we had forgotten his birthday. There was no special breakfast, decorations, or special birthday dinner—on the specific day of his birth. In our family, it is customary that on the actual birthday we make a big deal by celebrating them in a big way. However, I thought that since we'd celebrated all weekend that would suffice, and it wouldn't matter that we had timed our celebration for a different day. But in my son's eyes and heart, a tradition is a tradition; something he had counted on happening.

For me it was an epic fail day because my son spent some of his twelfth birthday in tears. He understood what I tried to do and was thankful after all, but my Mommy heart was sad that he spent even a moment of his special day crying. He realized there will be days like this in life when we expect certain things to happen but they don't. The overall lesson was that God allows these types of days in our lives to teach us something. Not necessarily a punishment of sorts, but more of a message that we won't always get what we want in life and we will have to be all right with that.

In a society that lacks traditions and family time, it is important to make room for such things. Your child will not care how much money your household has, how many pairs of shoes he has, or even how many vacations he goes on, but he will never forget how a particular event made him feel. Think about one of your favorite experiences from your childhood. For me it was

> Your child will not care how much money your household has, how many pairs of shoes he has, or even how many vacations he goes on, but he will never forget how a particular event made him feel.

my thirteenth birthday. My dad packed me and a bunch my neighborhood friends into the car and took us to a drive-in movie. We saw "Can't Buy Me Love," starring a young Patrick Dempsey. After the movie, we headed to our favorite pizza joint and then home for an all-girls sleepover. It is one of my all-time favorite memories as a kid not because of what we did that night (although Patrick Dempsey is still one of my favorite actors), but because of the way I felt that night, surrounded by my closest friends and family. My parents went out of their way to make sure it was a memorable birthday and it sure was.

People will often forget what you have said, what you may have been wearing, or what you were driving. But people will never forget how a particular experience made them *feel*. This is why I encourage you to always be mindful of how you are making your son feel. Even on epic fail days, it's how you handle the situation and what message you impart that matters. The day my son forgot his shoes I could have yelled at him. Instead we got in the car and headed back home where they all played outside for the rest of the afternoon. The day I burned dinner, I could have blamed it on someone or something else that distracted me from cooking Instead I apologized and we laughed at how the pigeon (who lives in the ceiling fan of our patio) took off, probably afraid I was going to roast her, too. Finally, the day of my son's birthday fail I could have told him how ungrateful he was after all I had done for him over the weekend but instead I told him I was sorry and I would never break a tradition again. Those choices have turned events that could have been disasters into warm and lasting memories instead—exactly the ones we want to make with our sons.

What Matters Most: Things to Do

- Write one good thing that occurred on an epic fail day and put it into a mason jar to share later.

- When an epic fail day occurs, turn it into a fun activity. Example: instead of going home with my kid without shoes, I should have headed to the park to let him play on the grass.

- Write down one way you will give yourself grace when you an encounter an epic fail day.

- Recount what you saw as an epic fail day with your kids and see how their perspective differs. Sometimes that's all you need to see the experience with new and grateful eyes.

Prayer

Lord,

May Your grace be sufficient for me when an epic fail day occurs. Remind me that Your strength is perfected in my weakness. Help me to see these epic fail days are a gift from You to slow down and enjoy the years I have with my son. Allow me to see these days as teachable moments from which my son may learn that he won't always get what he wants in life. Help me not to be so hard on myself, but rather give myself grace when I have experienced a tough day with my son. Grant me the strength to start fresh tomorrow, fully believing and trusting that You have equipped me with all I need to be an excellent mother.

In Jesus name, Amen

How can a young person stay on the path of purity? By living according to your word.
Psalm 119:9

Encourage the Value of Purity

Usually when we hear the word purity we think of something unblemished, untouched, or free of contaminates. When we think of a gender remaining pure, our minds automatically connect that value with a woman. Why? Has society made us believe that only women can be pure? That is not the case at all. In the same manner that women lose their virginity, so do men. Why is it that women are considered unworthy if they lose their virginity before marriage, but men are considered to reach a level of manhood of sorts if they do?

As I researched this matter I found that men have just as much to lose as women do when they give in to the temptation of having sex with someone. Why is it important for our sons to remain pure until marriage? First, he will receive spiritual covering from your husband and you as he enters marriage. Second, he will receive a full blessing as he enters marriage with his spouse. Finally, the new couple receives their spiritual inheritance to be fruitful and multiply in their home.

This is the way I have explained purity to my boys: Your heart has been intended solely for your future spouse. However, every time you are with someone, you give them pieces of your heart. Therefore, what will you have left when you meet the person God intended for you to share life with? Will it be fair to the person who was supposed to have an entire heart to receive one that is fragmented, sick, hurt, or even mangled? Yes, we all enter marriage with some sort of baggage that needs to be dealt with, but what if the issue of purity is not one of them? Instead of thinking they are bound to get hurt, deceived or heartbroken, they would be free to love their spouses in limitless ways.

I love the story of Isaac and Rebekah because it speaks of a relationship that receives spiritual covering from Abraham and Sarah. Isaac and Rebekah receive the blessing from her family and in doing so, they receive the promise God gave Abraham that he would be as numerous as the stars. Even though Abraham sent his servant to select a maiden for Isaac, I would like to think that, as I discussed in the previous chapter, **Praying For His Helpmate**, Abraham's decision seems to be similarly motivated. When you've specifically prayed for your son's helpmate, I believe God will hand-pick that woman, because the Bible says so. Let's read the story found in Genesis 24 verses 1-15:

Abraham was now very old, and the Lord had blessed him in every way. He said to the senior servant in his household, the one in charge of all that he had, *"Put your hand under my thigh.* I want you to swear by the Lord, the God of heaven and the God of earth, that you will not get a wife for my son from the daughters of the Canaanites, among whom I am living, but will go to my country and my own relatives and get a wife for my son Isaac." The servant asked him, "What if the woman is unwilling to come back with me to this land? Shall I then take your son back to the country you came from?"*

"Make sure that you do not take my son back there," Abraham said. "The Lord, the God of heaven, who brought me out of my father's household and my native land and who spoke to me and promised me on oath, saying, 'To your offspring I will give this land'—he will send his angel before you so that you can get a wife for my son from there. If the woman is unwilling to come back with you, then you will be released from this oath of mine. Only do not take my son back there."

So, the servant put his hand under the thigh of his master Abraham and swore an oath to him concerning this matter. Then the servant left, taking with him ten of his master's camels loaded with all kinds of good things from his master. He set out for Aram Naharaim and made his way to the town of Nahor. He had the camels kneel down near the well outside the town; it was toward evening, the time the women go out to draw water.

Then he prayed, "Lord, God of my master Abraham, make me successful today, and show kindness to my master Abraham. See, I am standing beside this spring, and the daughters of the townspeople are coming out to draw water. May it be that when I say to a young woman, 'Please let down your jar that I may have a drink,' and she says, 'Drink, and I'll water your camels too'—let her be the one you have chosen for your servant Isaac. By this I will know that you have shown kindness to my master."

Before he had finished praying, Rebekah came out with her jar on her shoulder.

I love the fact that the servant had not finished praying when Rebekah walked onto the scene. He even prays that when he requests water from the maiden she will show him kindness and by that matter he will know she is the one God has chosen for His servant Isaac. Hear me when I tell you that God will show you who she is supposed to be, and for any young lady who is not supposed to walk life with him, my best recommendation is to pray for her too!

I remember the day my eldest son came home talking about a lovely young lady he had met and was interested in asking out to a movie. I asked him if he had prayed about this idea. He said he had not but he didn't see anything wrong with a movie and neither did I. However, since I knew her name I began praying for her. My prayer was simple: *Lord, if this is the girl You have picked for my son then I ask You to help them get to know each other better and find You leading them into a courtship.* They went to the movies and several other activities together before my son felt a tugging at his heart that this was not the person God had chosen for him. He sat at the kitchen table explaining to us how he couldn't waste her time, knowing that God had spoken to him. He didn't feel good about ending their friendship but he knew it was the right thing to do.

In Isaac and Rebekah's story it recounts that Rebekah received her blessing as she left home. In Genesis 24 verse 60, *And they blessed Rebekah and said to her, "Our sister, may you increase to thousands upon thousands, may your offspring possess the cities of their enemies."* Although it was said upon Rebekah, if Rebekah received it so did Isaac, because they would become one through marriage.

Just like Isaac and Rebekah received their blessing from both sides of the family, our sons know that there is a blessing that is theirs to receive if they enter marriage with the one God has selected for them and if they do so in a state of purity. We have stressed the importance of keeping their hearts, minds, and souls intact for the helpmate God has chosen for them.

> We have stressed the importance of keeping their hearts, minds, and souls intact for the helpmate God has chosen for them.

You may think this sounds old-fashioned, but think what heartaches could have been avoided for you and your spouse if someone thought of this profound blessing for you, and discussed it with you. Even if you have a wonderful marriage that you feel is God-given, don't you want to make sure your son has the same? In my life, I made a few bad dating decisions before meeting the man God destined for me. Because of that, I decided I wanted to stay ahead of the game when raising my sons.

Finally, we know that God made Abraham a promise in Genesis 26 verse 4, *I will make your descendants as numerous as the stars in the sky and will give them all these lands, and through your offspring all nations on earth will be blessed.*

Because we know Isaac is Abraham's son then he too would receive this promise from the Lord. He would multiply and make the land fruitful. What a blessing to think that our sons are equipped with this truth for life.

Whatever we instill in their hearts will become the truth by which they live by. So, I encourage you to have that difficult conversation that possibly no one ever had with you. Let him know how important it is to guard his purity for the woman God has selected for him. That she deserves to get a whole man and not one that needs mending because that isn't what God has intended. There is no greater way to walk into a marriage than in purity, gifting the couple with the spiritual covering, blessing, and inheritance their union merits.

What Matters Most: Things to Do

- Write down one way you will explain the importance of purity.

- Explain to your son what happens when you do not remain pure.

- Write down one way you can explain to him how he can overcome temptation when confronted with it.

Prayer

Lord,

I pray that my son will remain pure until You bring into his life the woman You have selected for him to marry. I pray that they enter the covenant of marriage in complete purity so that in turn they may receive spiritual covering from You. That because they remain pure they are able to receive a full blessing. That they will then also receive their inheritance to be fruitful and multiply in their home as Abraham did.

In Jesus name, Amen

*The tongue has the power of life and death,
and those who love it will eat its fruit.*
Proverbs 18:21

Speak to Him with Intention

They say that people are a product of their environment, but I'd like to suggest the opposite—people are a product of environments they never want to experience again. That was the case for me when I began to have children of my own. I decided very early that I didn't want our children to hear the things that I had once heard spoken over me. I became intentional about speaking in life, speaking in love, speaking to build, and speaking to bless them and their future generations.

Why did I think this was so important? Because as the Word of God says, "there is power" in the tongue. Such a small vessel, one that can either cause great joy or great sorrow in a person's life, but one that you will most definitely eat the fruit of. The words you say can and do come back to haunt you later in life,

> The words you say can and do come back to haunt you later in life, so it's important to be intentional about them, and teach your children to do the same.

so it's important to be intentional about them, and teach your children to do the same.

One day my second son came home from school with an English assignment and requested my help. We sat at the kitchen table, trying to figure it out together. I tried my best to explain the assignment the way I understood it, but neither one of was getting anywhere. My son seemed confused and frustrated. He looked at me and said, "I know, Mom, I'm just dumb."

Sadness filled me. How could he think that of himself? I immediately told him how far from the truth that statement was, and began to give him reasons why it was a lie and why he shouldn't believe nor repeat it again. As his mom, I realized he needed me to be his cheerleader and as such, I wouldn't allow him to dump disheartening words on himself.

The Bible says in Deuteronomy 34 verse 17, *They are not just idle words for you—they are your life.* How can you speak spiritual life into your son's life? Simple. Speak the Word of God over him.

Here are some of my favorite verses.

That person is like a tree planted by streams of water, which yields its fruit in season and whose leaf does not wither— whatever they do prospers. Psalm 1:3

The words I have spoken to you—they are full of the Spirit and life. John 6:63

My mouth will speak words of wisdom. Psalm 49:3

When I was studying elementary education, they gave us a handout of positive statements we could say to our students. They were great little one-liners but I began to think about ways to take that message further. What if I spoke this way all the time to my boys? What if I was intentional in speaking with love towards them? I began researching Bible verses I could use as the basis for the messages I would use throughout their youth.

Here are some of them:

Jeremiah 31:3a says, *I have loved you with an everlasting love;*	My statement became: I love you with an everlasting love!
Philippians 1:9 says, *and this is my prayer: that your love may abound more and more.*	My statement became: I love you more!!
Psalm 59:16a says, *But I will sing of your strength, in the morning I will sing of your love;*	My statement became (in my best "Elf" singing voice): I love you! I love you! I love you!

When my son was about six years old, we were in a store when he threw a full-blown tantrum when he didn't get a particular toy he wanted. I kid you not it was as though I was looking at myself at the very same age throwing the exact same tantrum with one of my parents. I remained calm and asked God to give me wisdom at that moment. Behind me, I heard someone say, "You are paying for your own actions."

Was I? Could I have chosen different actions, different words and helped my son before it got to this point? Instead of taking that person's statement as a criticism, I saw it as a challenge to ask God to allow me to see and help manifest something different in my son's life. I asked God for the words that would build him into a man of character. Here are some of the verses I've used for my sons:

But I (insert your son's name) am like an olive tree flourishing in the house of God. Psalm 52:8

And the boy (insert your son's name) continued to grow in stature and in favor with the Lord and with people. 1 Samuel 2:26

God gave (insert your son's name) wisdom and very great insight, and a breadth of understanding as measureless as the sand on the seashore. 1 Kings 4:29

I saw the evidence of how words can create a great adult man when I was thirteen. We were visiting family in another country and I was riding in the back seat of a pickup truck. We stopped at an intersection and a man in a military uniform walked towards the truck. My grandmother stepped out to greet him. He got on his knees before her and she paused, speaking a blessing over him. I was in total shock and wondered why this was man kneeling before my grandmother.

What had she done to earn that kind of respect and deference from him? She later told me that he was a nephew who always asked for her prayers of blessing as he traveled with the military. That day is seared in my heart because it was the moment I realized the immense power of words, and specifically words for a young man.

I have tried to live by my grandmother's example in the years since. Here are some of the blessings I've found to speak over my sons:

I will make you into a great nation, and I will bless you; I will make your name great, and you will be a blessing. Genesis 12:2

All these blessings will come on you and accompany you if you obey the Lord your God. Deuteronomy 28:2

Surely you have granted him unending blessings and made him glad with the joy of your presence. Psalm 21:6

Remember, when you speak to your son, what you invite into his life will come to pass. Those words will lead your son's course. I have always tried to speak aloud the miracles I wanted to see manifest in my sons' lives. My sons are not perfect, but they are growing into the men God intended them to be, and I am honored and humbled to be a small part of that.

Our words can cause growth in every area of our sons' lives, or they can cause decay which will, in turn, stunt their emotional, mental and spiritual growth. Remember, Mom: speak life, speak in love, speak to build, and speak blessings into their hearts!

What Matters Most: Things to Do

- For every negative statement, you make about your son, substitute three positive statements. Don't say "You are so stubborn". Instead, say you are determined. You are passionate. You are persevering.

- Write one Bible verse about speaking in love on an index card and say it out loud every morning.

- Write one Bible verse about speaking a blessing on an index card and say it out loud every evening.

Prayer

Lord,

Thank You for showing me that there is life and death in the words that I speak towards my son. Give me Your word to speak life into his. Give me Your love to speak love into his heart. Give me Your wisdom to build him into the man he needs to be. Give me Your blessing to speak blessings over him in this life and for his generations to come.

In Jesus name, Amen

And we know that in all things God works for the good of those who love him, who have been called according to his purpose.
Romans 8:28

What Matters Most of All

My sons have been the most amazing part of this adventure we get to call life. Countless stories, countless tears, but much more countless love. I realized shortly after having my first son that there was more to the experience of motherhood than just being his mom. God was actually using him to teach me the lessons I needed, in those specific areas where He needed to reach my heart. Eighteen years and five children later; and each one of them has taught me something invaluable.

So, What Matters Most of All? I would have to say those lessons that have worked the rugged edges of my heart, healed my soul, and brought me to experience life through His eyes. Each one of my children came with a lesson plan instead of an instructional manual. It all began with the message of unconditional love. God in His ingenious ways wanted me to experience unconditional love so that I in turn could understand

> My first son taught me just that, to love unconditionally like God loves us, regardless of our mistakes.

His love for me. My first son taught me just that, to love unconditionally like God loves us, regardless of our mistakes. No strings attached, pure, and full of an abundant life. God sees us as that pure unbroken baby, full of hopes, dreams, and expectation from us.

My second son taught me to find courage in the Lord. Fear was something I struggled with ever since I could remember. When my son began to struggle with it as well, I found ways to help him by reciting scripture. In doing so, I realized God was trying to heal me of that same fear. Through prayer, God gave me courage. Courage to overcome the past. Courage to allow Him to heal my heart. Courage to step forth into the future of good He had prepared for me. It was an amazing journey of freedom. I now believe in my heart the verse *thou shalt not fear* because I'm convinced He is with me always.

My third son taught me patience. The kind of patience a farmer exercises as he waits for his crops to yield their fruit. The patience to raise my boys intentionally during those busy years. The patience to know that one day they would grow up and those trying moments would become fleeting memories. The patience to see the fruit yield in their lives with all the lifelong Biblical lessons I had prayed for. Through them, I began to understand that Mother was the best title I could ever gain on this earth. And in them,

I gained patience to allow Him to work out what needed to be dealt with in my heart for my calling and to His Glory.

My fourth son taught me peace; the peace that surpasses all understanding. The peace that only He can give me so I know that He loves my children more than I do. The peace that He has plans to prosper and bring good into their lives. The peace to know He is in control of my life, and of those I love and care for.

My sons have brought me years of goodness, joy, and faithfulness. For that I am eternally grateful to my Heavenly Father. And that, to me, is what matters most of all—the wonderful lessons He has taught me through the children I have been blessed to raise.

> And that, to me, is what matters most of all—the wonderful lessons He has taught me through the children I have been blessed to raise.

What Matters Most: Things to Do

To find what matters most of all, try these suggestions:

- ➤ Write down one thing you know you need God to deal with in your heart

- ➤ What thing could God be using in your child's life to teach you something new?

- ➤ How will you apply this lesson in every area of your life?

- ➤ Can you share those lessons with your children, and help them see the power of God in their lives?

Prayer

Lord,

Reveal to me anything in my heart that is hindering Your perfect will in my life. Show me in what ways my son is a tool in Your hand to deal with this area. Show me how I should apply what You teach me to every area of my life. Let me have a teachable spirit so that it can be used for my purpose and Your Glory.

In Jesus name, Amen.

About the Author

Founder of Strong and Courageous Women, Inc., Francis has been called to service. She is committed to serving other women and bringing hope, life, and a reflection of Christ into their everyday lives. This commitment led to the creation of *Strong and Courageous Women* Magazine. She serves as editor-in-chief of the magazine and is also one of the equity partners at NOW SC Press.

Francis knows her biggest job is being a mother. Married fifteen years with five children, she walks her journey daily with God, family, and work.

God is able to do far more than we could ever ask for or imagine. He does everything by his power that is working in us. Galatians 3:20

To Contact the Author:

Email: francis@strongandcourageouswomen.com
www. Facebook.com/StrongandCourageousWomen
Website: StrongAndCourageousWomen.com

A Day in the Life

My day usually begins before the sun is up; often with a piping hot cup of coffee and a journal. I sit in that cozy corner of my sofa, my legs covered by a fuzzy blanket, and begin to pray. I pray and quietly write down the things God talks to me about pertaining to my life, family, and the things He's called me to do. After about thirty minutes, I pick up whatever book I'm currently reading and dive into the next chapter or two.

By this time my middle school boys are up and following the same prayer routine. When they're done, they start their school day routine by getting dressed and preparing their own lunches. At the same time, my husband makes himself a quick breakfast and runs out the door with them to take them to school on his way to work. It's now time to get the preschooler and grade schooler ready for their day. I make breakfast, get them dressed, scoot them to the bathroom where they brush their teeth and comb their hair. They get their shoes on and wait on the couch for mommy to get ready.

We grab backpacks, I grab my premade breakfast protein shake, briefcase, and shoes and run out the door to load everyone in the minivan. Nine times out of ten, I realize in the van that I have forgotten the dog, so I run back in to give her water, feed her and make sure she goes to the potty before I finally leave to drop off the preschooler and then the grade schooler.

For the few minutes, I'm finally alone in the car, I either enjoy the silence or call a friend to pray with. My business day starts when I arrive at the office. Each day is different, filled with meetings to discuss future publishing clients or *Strong Courageous Women* magazine-related items. After five hours or so at the office, I wrap things up, then scurry back to pick up the two youngest children.

We all arrive home around the same time and the house is noisy as we discuss the day, homework assignments they may have, and books they will read before bed. We change our clothes, wash our hands, and make snacks. Once everyone has finished with their snacks and are settled, I return to the kitchen table to work for a bit while the middle schoolers finish their homework. The grade schooler and preschooler usually put together puzzles, color, or play cooking. I usually work at the kitchen table because if the children need me I'm close enough to take a break and assist them with their homework.

As dinnertime nears, the older boys finish their homework and head outside to play with their siblings and friends while I prep the kitchen and cook dinner. Dinner is usually ready by the time my husband walks in from work. They all come in, wash up, settle into their places and take a rare moment to quiet down as we say grace.

There's tons of conversation and noise, but sitting around that dinner table is my favorite part of the day. I've cried, thinking of the day that it will be empty, when all my children will be grown up and moved into to their own homes with their wives and children.

The older boys are in charge of the dishes and trash, as I start bedtime routines with the little ones. I get them showered, and in their pajamas; then we read for thirty minutes, say our prayers and the younger ones are off to bed. The middle schoolers are usually showered as well by this time. I walk into their respective rooms, say a prayer, and give them a hug and a kiss.

It's the end of their day but the start of the second half of mine. I use this time to catch up with my husband as we do laundry, prep anything needed for the next day at school, and sometimes accomplish some more tasks for work.

Usually by eleven I'm finally able to slip into bed with an extremely grateful heart, thankful for all that God provides daily for me and my family. I remind

Him how much I love Him, how grateful I get to be a mom to these children, and even though I'm exhausted on most days, as Proverbs 31:25 says, *She is clothed with strength and dignity; she can laugh at the days to come.*

Will you share your ...

"Day in the Life?"

Go to www.nowscpress.com/DITL

- Enter your Day to share with our mom community
- Enter to win a Starbucks card

One $10 Starbucks card per month.

Your entry stays eligible for the length of the contest.

Because we think every mom deserves a free cup of coffee every once in a while!

#SCWLife #WMMCrayon

Look for our other titles at www.nowscpress.com including What Matters Most of All: My Calendar is Written in Crayon, Smart Advice for Working Single Moms. In the meantime, enjoy this short excerpt!

Abby

When it comes, it hits you like a ton of bricks.

Bam. You're a divorced, single mom. And boy, is it sneaky. It even got to me reading my car insurance policy: Abby Brundage, a divorced woman, will be 37 on … Thanks for the reminder, State Farm! Your marriage failed, but you're all paid up for the next six months!

You think the day you sign the divorce papers is when the identity crisis starts, but it's not. This is merely the day the key goes into the lock that opens the door and welcomes in the parade of surprises; that will make you wonder who you are now that you're not the Mrs. you thought you'd always be.

It took me a long time to be able to say the word "ex-husband." Isn't it strange how identifying someone else seems to say so much about yourself? Saying I have an ex-husband was like rolling out a banner scribbled with labels about myself: Inadequate. Disposable. Unattractive. Imperfect. While the identity I always wanted was sent into a tailspin, there was this new me being involuntarily created.

I wanted to ignore this new person, whoever she was, but I knew deep down she had potential for greatness. I didn't want to know her, because to acknowledge her would mean I was accepting this new identity. If I could play ostrich and not look at the single mom in the mirror maybe I could convince other people I was better than that. Better than the stereotype I thought summarized the life and appearance of the divorced mother. But while I was busy avoiding her, I also had a glimmer of hope that she was somehow a better version of myself. To unveil her, I still had to navigate some waters of uncertainty.

Last Christmas, I scrolled through Pinterest for ideas to decorate my house – the house I proudly bought on my own to start over with my sons. All the merriment came to a halt when I checked out decorations for the front door. The monogram seemed to be this season's hot item. A simple wooden letter decorated with bows, polka dots, burlap, or whatever suits your style. I loved the idea until I started thinking about what letter I'd choose. My maiden name? It's not my sons'. My married name? It just didn't feel like mine anymore, and it hurt too much to claim it. Nothing felt right. The decoration was so insignificant, yet it really spoke to who I was. What was my name now?

Just like the letter on the front door, many of the things that send us spiraling into this identity crisis exist only on the outside. Truth does not stem from external matters. God says that we need to look inside to see what really matters and know who we are.

One day, I took my boys to Magic Kingdom. Our first stop was a photo op. with Mickey Mouse. This was our first family photo with Mickey and our first one post-divorce. We posed, smiling; the perfect image the photographer wanted. But as we rounded the corner into the gift shop to purchase the photo, I broke down in tears. I had imagined that first Disney family photo for years, but never thought this was how it would look. A single mom holding an eight-month-old and a toddler. Whose family and life was this?

I tried to hide my face from my boys and put on a smile. My older son, two years old at the time, looked at the photo, then up at me, beaming. "Are we going home now?"

Just as he didn't understand there was so much more left to see in the magical world of Disney, I realized I had been missing the point, worrying about door decorations and family photos. Home to my son was wherever we were. That identity hadn't changed. And neither had mine. I was still myself, still a mom, and still building a home – not the one I had imagined years before – but still a home filled with love, warmth, and memories.

And more importantly, I am more than the salutation on the insurance policy, the polka dot letter on the door, or even the family photo with Mickey. I am Mom, and I am able to love my children more deeply than anyone on this earth. These two gifts that God gave me have allowed me to love and be loved in a way that fills my heart on a daily basis.

If you're now checking the "divorced" box you never used to give a second glance to, or juggling a shared custody schedule that was never supposed to be on your calendar, remember the labels the world gives you are not nearly as important as the one God did. You are His child and He entrusted those little ones to you. Remind yourself of that on a daily basis, and you'll find the same key that unlocked a door to an identity crisis can also open the door to a new world of sweet, warm memories and unconditional love.

What Matters Most: To Do List

If you are struggling with finding your identity post-divorce, try some of these tips:

- Take a sheet of paper and write at the top: "I'm Proud to be …" and every day add one thing to describe yourself.

- Is there something about your identity as a single mom that you've been avoiding? Something you're ashamed of? Pray or journal about that.

- Schedule a photo session for you and your kids. Create new family photos. If you want, wear Spanx and fake eyelashes. They'll make you feel even more gorgeous than you already are!

- Make a list of the things that set you apart from every other woman. Are you a wonderful singer or great baker? These are the things that people will remember about you.

- Support groups can be great for helping you through these new, uncharted waters. Look for one near you to find other single moms who can understand and support you.

Buy the What Matters Most of All: My Calendar is Written in Crayon book now at www.nowscpress.com/crayon

www.ingramcontent.com/pod-product-compliance
Lightning Source LLC
Chambersburg PA
CBHW070621300426
44113CB00010B/1613